CHRISTIANITY THE MODERN WORLD
FOR GCSE

MICHAEL KEENE

John
HUNT
Publishing

Copyright © 2000 John Hunt Publishing Ltd

Text © 2000 Michael Keene

Photographs © Alex Keene

ISBN 1 903019 58 3

Designed by
ANDREW MILNE DESIGN

Write to John Hunt Publishing Ltd
46a West Street, Alresford, Hampshire SO24 9AU, UK

The rights of Michael Keene as author and Alex Keene as photographer of this work
have been asserted in accordance with the Copyright, Designs and Patents Act 1988.

A CIP catalogue record for this book is available from the British Library.

Printed in Malaysia

Note: Throughout the series BCE [Before Common Era] and CE [Common Era]
have been used in place of the more Common BC and AD although they mean the same.

Biblical quotations taken from:
The New International Version. Hodder and Stoughton.

CONTENTS

1:1 Being Human

One book in the Bible stands out with a different message to all the others – a message largely of despair. It is the book of Ecclesiastes in the Old Testament and you can get a flavour of what it has to say about being human by reading 1.1–11 and 3.1–8. The message of the book can be summed up simply –human beings are born, live for a short while and then die. Unlike the world in which they live which seems to go on for ever human beings die – and are soon forgotten. In the opinion of this unknown author life can be summed up in one word – meaningless [see box 1].

The Bible's picture

The Bible gives us two sides to the human picture:
1] "By the sweat of your brow you will eat your food until you return to the ground since from it you were taken; for dust you are and to dust you will return." *[Genesis 3.19]*. All human life on earth is like grass blossoming 'like a wild flower in the meadow' until the wind passes over it – and it is gone for ever [box 2].
2] "When I consider your heavens, the work of your fingers, the moon and the stars, which you have set in place, what is man that you are mindful of him, the son of man that you care for him? You made him a little lower than the angels and crowned him with glory and honour." *[Psalm 8.4,5]*. Human beings have been made in the image of God with God-given responsibilities to care for the world in which they live *[Genesis 1.27]*. With the great gifts that human beings have been given come great responsibilities as well. They are stewards, placed on earth by God to care for it.

The truth about human beings probably lies somewhere in between the two. Human beings are more important than the grass in the field and at times they are almost god-like.

> **BOX 1**
>
> **ECCLESIASTES 1.2**
>
> *Meaningless! Meaningless! says the Teacher. Utterly meaningless! Everything is meaningless.*

At other times, though, they are capable of acting with great stupidity and ignorance.

Spiritual beings

From the moment that we are born a life-long learning process begins. This begins in our family, where we have our earliest learning experiences, but soon friends, teachers and the mass media begin to influence us more and more. Religion, too, can have a considerable influence. Christian parents take their children to their local church where they learn certain spiritual 'truths', amongst which are that:
1] God created the world in which they live.
2] God created all human life, giving to each individual those characteristics which make them special – even unique.
3] Human beings have spiritual as well as physical and emotional needs. Each human being has a soul [spirit] as well as a body. To be a complete person the spiritual must not be neglected and this involves worshipping God. This is where the place of worship and the worshipping community become very important for many people

Each of these spiritual 'truths' will crop up time and time again throughout this book. Many

 Talk it over

Are there times when you agree with the writer in the Old Testament who said that the whole of life is meaningless. What kind of experiences lead you to think like that? Do you think that life is meaningless in the end?

Work to do

1 Which two sides of human nature are presented in the Bible?

2 a. How do human beings learn what is expected of them as they grow up into adults?

b. What 'truths' does religion teach?

c. Are you happy with the idea that human beings have spiritual as well as physical and emotional faculties? What leads you to believe that you have a soul or spirit as well as a body?

> **BOX 2**
>
> **PSALM 103.14-16**
>
> *He knows how we are formed, he remembers that we are dust.*
> *As for man, his days are like grass, he flourishes like a flower of the field; the wind blows over it and it is gone, and its place remembers it no more.*

people, of course, leave their Christian feelings and beliefs behind them as they grow up. Others come to believe in Christ, and take on board the principles that he taught, later in life. Some carry their religious faith with them from childhood through adulthood into old age. A Christian faith not only affects what we believe but also the way that we live and behave. It influences the decisions that we make and the way that we treat other people. Before we move on, though, to see how this works out in practice it is important to look at the part that relationships with others play in the lives of all human beings. [unit 1.2].

[A] The Christian faith teaches that all human beings are born with a sinful nature. Do you agree with this?

1:2 Human Relationships

KEY QUESTION

How IMPORTANT ARE OTHER PEOPLE IN OUR LIVES?

John Donne, the 16th century poet, wrote: 'No man is an island, entire of itself'. Christianity teaches us that each person has been created by God to grow as an individual – physically, spiritually and emotionally. Jesus said as much in his parable of the sower [box 1]. Seeds, given the right conditions, will always grow but there is no growth without a struggle. So it is with human beings.

[A] How is the relationship of this child with its mother and father going to change as it grows older?

Our first important relationships are with our parents, mother and father. For the nine months that we grow in our mother's womb the relationship between mother and baby is one of complete dependence. She provides us with everything that we need to survive. The nature of that dependence slowly changes when we are born and begin to grow but, to begin with, it remains almost total [B]. It is only when we begin to form strong attachments to other people [brothers, sisters, friends etc] that we become gradually less dependent on our parents.

Primary and secondary relationships

At every stage in our lives we form relationships with other people. Some of these are very strong and life-enhancing. Others are less important and passing. All of them fall into one of two groups:

1] Primary Relationships These are the relationships on which we build our lives. To begin with they centre around our family but they later expand to include school friends and, later still, those with whom we work. For most of us our relationship with our husband or wife [spouse] will be the most important that we will make. These relationships arouse strong feelings in us and we find ourselves, through them, drawn into the highs and lows of other peoples' lives. Successful primary relationships can bring us great joy but

BOX 1

MATTHEW 22.34-40

Hearing that Jesus had silenced the Sadducees, the Pharisees got together. One of them, an expert in the law, tested him with this question: 'Teacher, which is the greatest commandment in the Law?' Jesus replied: ' Love the Lord your God with all your heart and with all your soul and with all your mind.' This is the first and greatest commandment. And the second is like it: 'Love your neighbour as yourself'.

1 Read the quotation in box 1.
   a. Which two relationships is Jesus describing here?
   b. What are we saying is we describe these two relationships as 'primary'?
   c. What do you think it means in practice to love God and to love one's neighbour?
   d. Why do you think that Jesus brought together the need to love God and to love one's neighbour?

2 a. What is a primary relationship?
   b. What is a secondary relationship?
   c. Describe TWO differences between a primary and a secondary relationship?

unsuccessful ones can be extremely painful. Either way, though, these relationships play a very important part in our growth as human beings.
2] Secondary Relationships There are many people who play a less than central part in our lives. They may be casual acquaintances, people from the street on which we live [neighbours] or those that we work with. Some touch our lives for a short time and then move on. Others stay longer but only remain on the fringes.

Changing relationships

Close relationships make their own demands on us and these may change over time. The relationship between parents and child is a very good example of this. To begin with the relationship is one of total dependency but as children grow older so they take more and more responsibility for their own lives. Adjustments have to be made by both parents and children to take this into account - and this may sometimes be a painful experience. Almost every parent finds it difficult to adjust to the increasing demands for independence made by a growing adolescent whilst teenagers are not always the most reasonable people on God's earth!

One of the most difficult things to come to terms with is the increasing complexity of life. At the same time as hormones are roaring around within school and friends make increasing demands on all of us. We may turn to both for advice at times but they are unlikely to agree! All the time, though, we are working our way towards replacing the dependency of childhood with the inter-dependence of adult relationships.

Inter-dependence is the key to all adult relationships - whether between parents and children, between friends or in sexual relationships. It is only then that the marks of a true friendship between equals - love, trust, caring and respect - can grow. Even within a true friendship growth continually takes place. There is a world of difference between the friendship which leads to marriage and the friendship which grows after many

years of married life. If the friendship between two people does not grow over the years then it withers away. Growth is not always a comfortable or pleasant experience but it is essential.

When Jesus was asked by one of the Pharisees which of the many commandments in the Jewish law was the most important he replied that there were two relationships that really mattered [box 1]. The first is to love God with our whole being. The second is to love our neighbour as much as we love ourselves. In speaking like this Jesus was emphasising the two relationships which are at the centre of every Christian's life.

[B] This baby is totally dependent on its mother but why is this primary relationship so important to the mother?

1:3 | Making Moral Decisions

Everyone is continually faced with the need to make moral choices. A moral choice is one that forces us to choose between when we think to be right and wrong in any situation. Sometimes the moral choice is a clear one but more often than not the choice is blurred at the edges. As we grow older so these choices become more complex and difficult to make.

Looking for help

Many people look to the Christian Churches for help in making their moral decisions. There are many different Churches and the advice they give on moral issues often conflicts. The Churches follow two different approaches on such matters:

1] The Roman Catholic approach The Roman Catholic Church teaches that divine guidance on a whole range of moral issues has been given to human beings. This guidance can be found from:

a. The Bible. This book was completed two thousand years ago but it gives advice to Christians on a whole range of moral issues – including marriage, divorce, homosexuality and women leaders in the Church. The teaching of the Bible on these issues cannot change. Once laid down it is binding for ever. So, for instance, the Bible teaches that the marriage bond is unbreakable, that divorce is against the will of God, that the priesthood should be all-male and that homosexuality is against the natural law of God. The Church has a duty to explain what

the Bible has to say on these issues – but it cannot change or dilute it.

b. Church teaching and the Pope. Some moral issues – such as abortion, contraception and euthanasia – were unknown at the time that the Bible was written. God makes his will known on these issues through Church Councils which draw together all the bishops under the leadership of the Pope. Church Councils are only held very occasionally, just three since the 16th century, but the Pope can speak infallibly on certain issues. The Pope is much more likely, however, to make his mind known through writing an encyclical [papal document] in which he explains the Church's position on particular issues. Sometimes this teaching is very controversial as the encyclical issued by Pope Paul VI on contra-ception in 1968 ['Humanae Vitae']. A papal encyclical places Roman Catholics under a very strong moral obligation to obey its teaching.

2] The Protestant approach Protestants believe that the Bible, the Word of God, is the sole source of authority that God has given to the human race.

[A] Do you think that moral advice given in the Bible necessarily applies to life today? Explain your answer.

BOX I

EXODUS 20.1-17

I am the Lord your God, who brought you out of Egypt, out of the land of slavery... You shall have no other gods before me... You shall not make yourself an idol... You shall not misuse the name of the Lord your God... Remember the Sabbath Day by keeping it holy... Honour your father and mother... You shall not murder... You shall not commit adultery... You shall not steal... You shall not give false testimony against your neighbour... You shall not covet.

Talk it over

How do you think that people who do not have a belief in God to guide them make their moral choices?

When the Bible gives direct teaching on moral issues that teaching must be obeyed because it expresses the will of God. The Ten Commandments [box 1] are an example of this. In other areas there are general principles in the Bible which individuals must apply to actual moral decisions. An example is this is the Golden Rule [see box 2]. This Rule should act as a guide in all moral decisions that Christians face.

The Ten Commandments and the Golden Rule

The Ten Commandments are a list of obligations towards God and fellow human beings that Moses was given by God on Mount Sinai. The Ten Commandments were actually included amongst a total of 613 laws, some negative and some positive, that were to govern Jewish personal and social life. These laws, known to Jews as the Torah, have governed the lives of Jews ever since they were first given around 1200 BCE. Although Jesus simplified the demands of the Ten Commandments with his 'Golden Rule' he did not at any time suggest that the Ten Commandments were redundant.

> **BOX 2**
>
> **MATTHEW 7.12**
>
> *So in everything, do to others what you would have them do to you, for this sums up the Law and the Prophets [the whole of the Jewish Scriptures].*

Most of the world's major religions have something similar to the Golden Rule. Jesus taught his followers that they were to show genuine care and love to everyone they met. The word 'agape' was used in the New Testament to describe this concern. It is usually translated 'love' but it does not mean what the word usually means today. It is an attitude of caring for all people, no matter who they are and what their needs might be. This concern must be at the heart of every moral decision that a Christian makes. You can find out more about agape love in unit 1.4.

 Work to do

1 Explain how:
a. A Roman Catholic
b. A Protestant
might seek to discover the will of God on moral issues.

2 a. List THREE moral issues on which a person might find advice in the Bible to help them decide what to do.
b. List THREE moral issues on which the Bible does not give specific moral advice.

3 Look at the Ten Commandments in box 1.
a. Which of these commandments do you think has relevance today?
b. Which commandments do you think has no relevance to life today? Explain the reasons for your choice in each case.

[B] Do you think that people might find the conflicting advice of different Churches on moral issues confusing? Would you expect a single Christian position on all moral decisions. Explain your answer, one way or the other.

1:4 Love

Properly used, the word 'love' conveys many feelings which show that human beings have a spiritual as well as a physical dimension to their personalities. Christians believe that, at one end of the scale, human beings may be related to animals but, at the other, they can enjoy communion with God. This makes human beings unique. When they treat the whole of creation, including their fellow human beings, lovingly they are behaving as God intended. To act without love and care, though, is to act inhumanely.

[A] How would you describe the special love that exists between parent and child?

Real love

The Christian teaching about love is very clear. You can find three quotations from the Bible of the true meaning of love in [boxes 1,2 and 3]. Love is the greatest, and most important, of all the virtues. As Paul wrote when discussing the three great Christian virtues of faith, hope and love: "The greatest of them all is love." Paul also said that if someone has all the other virtues, including faith and hope, yet does not have love, he or she is nothing: "I may have faith enough to move mountains, but if I have no love, I am nothing." [1.Corinthians 13.2]

Paul is merely emphasising what Jesus himself had said about love. He told his disciples that they must always put the needs of others before their own. They should not look for any return on the love that they showed. As Jesus said in the collection of sayings known as the Sermon on the Mount: "If you love only those who love you what reward can you expect? There must be no limit to your goodness, as your heavenly father's goodness knows no bounds." [Matthew 5.46-48]. Jesus summed up the demand that God makes on everyone:"Love the Lord your God with all your heart, and with all your soul, and with all your strength, and with all your mind; and your neighbour as yourself." [Luke 10.27]

This introduces us to another theme in the teaching of Jesus about love. We should love God, we should love our neighbour and we should love ourselves. In Christian terms this means loving ourselves as Christ loved us, seeing ourselves as Christ saw us and giving ourselves to others as Christ gave himself for us. As John wrote in the New Testament: "This is what love really is: not that we have loved God, but that he loved us and sent his Son as a sacrifice to atone for our sins. If God thus loved us, my dear friends, we must also love one another." [1.Jn 4.10,11].

An important early Church leader,
Augustine, said:
"Love God and do what you will."
What do you think he meant?

1 Explain the importance of love for Christian believers.

2 What is different about Christian love - agape?

3 "It is important to love your neighbour as you love yourself." Do you agree with this statement? Explain your answer.

4 Explain the difference between the four kinds of love.

5 Do you agree that love is the greatest, and the most important, of the three virtues?

[B] What do Christians believe to have been the supreme expression of the love of God?

True love

In the world of Jesus and Paul four different words were used to express the breadth of meaning found in the word 'love'. They were:

1] Eros - a love which is simply based on physical attraction and from which our word 'erotic' is derived. This word is not used at all in the New Testament.

2] Philos - a love for those people who are close to us, our family and friends.

3] Storge - the warm affection that we may have for a place that has special meaning for us.

4] Agape - Christian love, a reflection of the love that God has for us. This includes loving people to whom we do not feel particularly attracted; people who do not respond with warmth to us and loving people that we do not like. This is the meaning which the word usually carries in the New Testament.

The most well-known description of agape love is that found in the letter that Paul wrote to the Christians in Corinth. You can discover from box 3 the characteristics of true Christian love. This is the love that Christians are called upon to share in making all of their moral decisions and choices. It is a love which selflessly places the needs of others in front of our own. As far as the Christian is concerned it is the love which must be at the heart of every moral decision which is made. It was certainly the kind of love that motivated Jesus throughout his ministry and during the course of his death.

BOX 3

1 CORINTHIANS 13.4-8

Love is patient and kind. Love envies no one, is never boastful, never conceited, never rude; love is never selfish, never quick to take offence. Love keeps no score of wrongs, takes no pleasure in the sins of others but delights in the truth. There is nothing love cannot face; there is no limit to its faith, its hope, its endurance. Love will never come to an end...

1:5 | Friendship

Children begin to form friendships with each other at a very early age. As they grow up these friendships change. Some friendships break up and fade away. Other relationships develop and become firm – sometimes lifelong – friendships.

Where do our friends come from?

We can, of course, make friends with anyone we choose – as long as they agree! It sounds a very haphazard business and in many ways it is. In other ways, though, we are attracted to some people and not to others. It is most likely that our friends will:

1] Live in the same neighbourhood as us. When we are young our friends are mostly introduced to us by our parents. Just as our parents are most likely to draw their own friends from a similar background to themselves so our friends are likely to come from the same background.

2] Have similar interests to us. Common interests often draw people together – the same club, organisation or church for instance. Many of our early friends will probably go the same school as us. Friends like being together and they often have a common interest which binds them closely to each other.

3] Share some of our beliefs and opinions. Most friendships which grow into lasting relationships are based on what two, or more, people have in common. Obviously this does not mean that friends agree on everything – there is always room in a healthy friendship for differences of opinion. At the same time there is a real 'meeting of minds' in friendships which last the pace.

Most Christians belong to a church and this is rather like a family in which all members look out for one another. The same happens with friends. Christians are taught that they must love their

friends but that is not enough – they must also love those who are their enemies.

Relationships breaking down

Some friendships last and others do not. All of them come under pressure from time to time. If they are able to withstand the pressure they emerge much the stronger but often they buckle, and fail, under the weight. Close friends often grow apart or move to different schools or areas. Sometimes, though, the break-up is more dramatic as a misunderstanding is blown out of all proportion or two close friends start to compete with each other. The envy by one person of another may be at the root of a friendship beginning to crumble. Even the closest friends find that once unkind words are said or they begin to drift apart it is very difficult to rebuild the relationship, no matter how hard they both try.

Children and young people should find none of this surprising. Just the same happens in relationships and friendships between adults. It happens in the closest of all friendships – marriage. A couple who may promise to live with each other 'till death us do part' when they stand before the altar at their marriage may put each other through the messiest of divorces a few years later. It is true generally that the more emotional energy which is invested in a friendship the greater the heartbreak if that friendship ends.

In the early Christian church there were many bitter disputes between people who should have loved one another. Some of the disputes were fundamental and went to the very heart of the Christian faith. Within a few years of the death of Jesus, for instance, the Church was split right down the middle over whether non-Jews [Gentiles] should be made to live like Jews, and obey the

BOX 1

MATTHEW 18.15-17

If your brother does wrong, go and take the matter up with him, strictly between yourselves. If he listens to you, you have won your brother over. But if he will not listen, take one or two others with you, so that every case may be settled on the evidence of two or three witnesses. If he refuses to listen to them, report the matter to the congregation; and if he will not listen even to the congregation, then treat him as you would a pagan or a tax-collector.

[A] What do you think that this young couple can do to try to make sure that their friendship deepens, and grows, in the coming years?

same laws, when they became Christians. The argument was fuelled by the fact that most of the early Christians were Jewish and they expected everyone else to behave as they did – because Jesus was a Jew. Close friends found themselves on opposite sides in this particular argument.

The early Christians recognised that even close friends could fall out with each other sometimes. To deal with these disputes they developed a simply procedure [see box 1]. Although these words have probably been put in the mouth of Jesus by later believers they do show us the way that people behaved in the Early Church. As you will see in box 2 Paul also had his own advice for those who needed an effective way of dealing with their own anger.

▶ Work to do

1 How do most of us choose our friends?

2 What factors can place a strain on a friendship.

3 What is the Biblical advice for dealing with quarrels or disagreements within a friendship?

4 List TEN qualities that you would expect to find in a good friend - explain why each of these qualities is important.

5 Read Proverbs 7.17; 18.24 and 27.6. Make notes on all the points that you find there about real friendship.

1:6 | Sex

KEY QUESTION

WHAT IS THE CHRISTIAN ATTITUDE TO SEX?

Our sexuality is a crucial part of our personalities. Because of its capacity to hurt others each society places strict controls on sexual behaviour, especially amongst young people. In this country it is illegal for anyone to have sex with a person who is under the age of sixteen- although 'the age of consent' varies in other countries. Surveys show that only 20% [1 in 5] of men and women are virgins when they marry with 50% losing their virginity before they reach their 18th birthday.

BOX 1

1 CORINTHIANS 7.9

Now to the unmarried and the widows I say: It is good for them to stay unmarried, as I am. But if they cannot control themselves, they should marry for it is better to marry than to burn with passion.

Sex and marriage

For most people sex is a precious and special part of their lives. At its best it is a unique way of showing the love and commitment which two people feel for each other. As such, it is best enjoyed within the context of caring and acting responsibly towards another person. For most Christians marriage is the only relationship within which this can happen.

When we talk about 'sex outside marriage' we are talking about one of two different situations:

1] Pre-marital sex This is sex which takes place between two people, neither of whom are married. Pre-marital sex can be within a stable, caring relationship or it can be casual sex between two people who barely know each other. It would be silly to suggest that the two situations raise the same moral questions. They clearly raise very different issues.

2] Extra-marital sex This is sex which takes place between two people, one or both of whom are married to someone else [adultery]. This is a situation, too, which can raise different moral questions. In one the married relationship[s] in question may be dead and finished whilst in the other it may be very much alive with children and a spouse involved.

Sex outside marriage

There are many reasons why sexual activity outside marriage has become so much more common in recent years:

1] Effective contraception is now available - for both married and unmarried couples to use. Two people can now be almost certain that an unwanted baby will not result from their sexual activity.

[A] The mass media are constantly throwing messages about sex at us. Do you think this is helpful or could it confuse many young people who are trying to make up their own minds about sex - and its responsibilities?

1 Look at the quotation from Paul in box 1.
a. Put what Paul is saying there in your own words.
b. Do you think that his argument is a good reason for someone marrying?

2 a. What is pre-marital sex?
b. What is extra-marital sex?
c. What is the Christian attitude to sex outside marriage?

3 "Having an affair does no harm as long as you are not found out." Do you think that a Christian might put this argument forward to justify their behaviour?

2] If contraception fails then an abortion will almost certainly be available. With the 'morning-after' pill which ends conception if taken within four days of sex by aborting the foetus, no-one needs to go through with a pregnancy that they do not want.

3] Fewer people expect their partners to be virgins when they marry them.

4] Fewer people accept the teachings of the Christian Church which have always been against sex before, and outside, marriage.

A high price is paid, though, by many people for promiscuous sexual activity. Sexually transmitted diseases, such as gonorrhoea and herpes, are on the increase. AIDS is spreading, more unwanted and unplanned babies are being conceived and thousands of marriages break up every year because one, or both, of the partners has been unfaithful. Casual and unprotected sex is a risky, and dangerous, business.

Most Christians would insist that sex outside the marriage relationship is wrong. Jesus frequently spoke out against fornication [pre-marital sex] and adultery. Christians believe that sex is a God-given way of expressing true love to be enjoyed within marriage.

Celibacy

Celibacy is a chosen way of life that excludes marriage and sex. It has been associated with the Roman Catholic Church, and its priests, for centuries. In the New Testament Paul was certainly unmarried and he commended the celibate state to those who wished to devote their lives fully to the service of God [see box 1]. In 1139 the Catholic Church decreed that all of its priests should be celibate - the only Church to make such a demand. Although there are many voices within the Roman Catholic Church demanding a change the present Pope, John Paul 11, has declared that the rule about celibacy will remain in place.

[B] Roman Catholic priests are celibate. What does this mean?

BOX 2

MARY CALDERONE

A girl plays at sex, for which she is not ready, because fundamentally what she wants is love; and a boy plays at love, for which he is not ready, because what he wants is sex.

Mark 3. 31-35

1:7 Family Life

In our society, as in almost every other, the family is the most important social unit. The exact form it takes varies but the family is found everywhere because it seems to meet the needs of people better than anything else. Broadly speaking the family can take one of two different forms:

1] THE EXTENDED FAMILY This is the form of family life reflected in the Bible and it is still found in many countries today. In an extended family several generations of the same family either live together under the same roof or very close to each other. The extended family is very important in those countries where the State does not look after the young or the old - they are cared for within the family.

2] THE NUCLEAR FAMILY This is the modern Western family which consists of just two generations - parents and children - living together. When the children grow up they move away to live elsewhere and start a nuclear family of their own.

Family arrangements

About 50% of the people in this country live in a nuclear family. The remainder live in a variety of different arrangements including:

1] Expanded families. Old people, the disabled and the mentally handicapped sometimes live together as a family.

2] Community life. Nuns and monks live together in a community. A few other religious groups do so as well.

3] Reconstituted family. When someone divorces and remarries they often bring their children with them into the new family.

4] Lone-parent family [see unit 8.] A family in which one parent is left to bring up a child on his or her own.

5] A childless family. Some couples choose not to have a family whilst others are infertile.

The importance of the family

Most people, including Christians, feel that family life is very important for everyone. There are four reasons for maintaining this:

a. We gain our sense of identity from the family we belong to - physical characteristics, name, values etc. If a child is adopted he or she will not inherit genetic characteristics from the parents but will take a lot more - name and values.

 **Talk it over**

Look at the advice given by Paul in
boxes 1 and 2. What do you think of it?

[A] What are the main problems that this family might
have to face as the children grow up?

b. It teaches us what behaviour is and is not
acceptable – a process called 'socialisation'.
This prepares us for the roles that we will be
expected to play when we grow up. It is
through the family that we initially learn what
is right and wrong.

c. Our family provides us with our first
experiences of 'bonding' – with our parents,
brothers, sisters and other relations. We work
out how to give, and receive, love. We learn how
to deal with our strongest feelings – of anger,
excitement, confusion etc– in a way that will
not destroy our relationships with others.

d. Family life is the way that our society looks
after the most vulnerable people – the young
and the old – and offers them security.

Religious education

No-one is quite sure how much the later religious
beliefs of a person depend on their childhood and
upbringing. Obviously religious adults can come
out of non religious backgrounds and vice versa.
The Christian religion does expect, though, the
deeply held beliefs of parents to be passed on to
their children – although they may later reject
them. Amongst the most successful ways of doing
this are for parents to:

1] Pray at home with their children and read the
Bible to them.

2] Take their children with them when they go to
church on Sundays. Many churches make special
arrangements for children but families worshipping
together is obviously a strong binding mechanism
on all of them.

3] Put Christian principles into operation in the
home. This involves showing kindness to other
people; exhibiting self-discipline; listening to
others, especially children;
forgiving the children
when they make mistakes;
caring for members of
the family when they are
ill; showing a warmth and
tenderness in dealings
with each other and
working for the good of
all family members.
Christians believe that
they can call on the help
and assistance of God in
creating the kind of
family atmosphere in
which all members can
grow and mature [see
boxes 1 and 2].

BOX 3

**BISHOPS AT THE
ROMAN CATHOLIC
SECOND VATICAN
COUNCIL**

*As it is the parents
who have given life
to their children, on
them lies the
gravest obligation
of educating their
family... It is the
duty of parents to
create a family
atmosphere inspired
by love and
devotion to God,
and their fellow-
men.*

 Work to do

1 a. What are the main functions of a
family?
b. What are the differences between an
extended family and a nuclear family?

2 Explain how being Christian might help
a couple to bring up their children.

3 "A Christian family needs to worship
together to stay together." Do you agree?

4 Describe and explain how a church
could have an important role to play in
the family life of its members.

5 Christians believe that parents are the
main educators of their children - at
least in the most important areas of life.
What do you think they mean by this?

1:8 | Lone-Parent Families

KEY QUESTION

WHICH PARTICULAR PROBLEMS ARE FACED BY FAMILIES IN WHICH THERE IS JUST ONE ACTIVE PARENT?

One of the most important changes in family life in the last thirty years has been the growth in lone-parent [single-parent] families in Great Britain. The total of such families has risen from 620,000 in 1971 through 750,000 in 1976 to more than 1,300,000 by the year 2000. Over 1,600,000 children under the age of 16 now live with a single parent - 1,300,000 with their mother and 300,000 with their father. This means that 1 in every five families with dependent children now have just one parent living with them.

Explanations

There are many reasons why a one-parent family may come into existence:

1] The woman becomes pregnant but does not wish, or is unable to, marry the father of her child [34% of all lone-parent families]. The woman does not want to have an abortion and so the only alternative is for her to bring up the child herself. The vast majority of women in this situation are under the age of twenty-five. 50% of lone-parent mothers on Income Support are aged between 20 and 29. Just 5% are aged between 16 and 19.

2] The mother or father dies whilst there are still

1 a. What is a 'lone-parent' family?
 b. How many lone parents are there in the United Kingdom?
 c. What are the different sets of situations that create lone parents?

2 What are the main problems which lone parents face in to-day's world?

3 Do you think that single mothers and single fathers face the same problems as they try to cope with their situation - or do they each have their own set of problems?

young children in the family [6%]. In this case it is more likely to be the father who dies and the mother who brings up the child/children on her own.

3] The husband or wife deserts their partner and leaves them to bring up any children [19%].

4] The husband and wife divorce [33%]. Unless there are unusual circumstances the mother in this situation is usually given custody of the children. One in every four marriages now ends in divorce and in many of these dependent children are involved. In 8% of lone-parents it is the father rather than the mother who is given responsibility for the children.

The problems of lone-parents

There is a strong link between lone-parents and poverty. Whilst some lone-parents receive strong help and support from their families the majority do not. They have to face the problems associated with bringing up children on their own, amongst which are:

1] Having young dependent children many lone-parents find that they cannot work full-time. It often proves to be financially out of the question for them to pay for a full-time child minder.

2] The State benefits available to them are barely sufficient to cover their basic needs . Surveys suggest that as many as 90% of lone-parents who do not work are living in real poverty.

3] Children have to suffer the long-term consequences of being brought up by just one parent. Most people agree that the ideal situation for bringing up children is to have two parents. As most lone-parent children are deprived of day-to-day contact with a father it is often boys who suffer most. Lone-parent children find that shortage of money in the family, and the constant worry that this brings, often has a devastating effect on family life.

[A] Do you think that a lone parent is better bringing up a child than two unhappy parents?`

4] In situations where the father is liable to pay maintenance the money is often not paid or, at best, irregularly. The Child Support Agency was set up in the early 1990s to compel absent fathers to support their ex-partners and children but, in many cases, this has only made the situation worse.

People who defend lone-parent families, and their rights, point out that the situation is only a temporary one for most of them. Statistics show that within five years most lone parents, especially women, will move in to cohabit or marry another partner. To help single parents in the United Kingdom cope with some of their immediate difficulties several organisations have been set up. Perhaps the most well-known of these is the Gingerbread Association for One-Parent Families which offers support to lone mothers and fathers.

BOX I

MICHAEL PORTILLO. MP. 1993

Over 8,000 girls under the age of 18 become pregnant every year in England and Wales, the equivalent of two in every secondary school. Our rate of teenage pregnancies is seven times higher than Holland and not I think because the British teenager is more likely to have premarital sex than her Dutch counterpart. And our rate of abortions is higher, too. Teenage pregnancies often lead to a whole life of state dependence with few luxuries. The question is what action could be taken by any of us to reduce the incidence of pregnancy among those not wishing or not ready to start a family.

1:9 Contraception [1]

Most Christians believe that having children is a primary purpose of marriage. The Catholic Church teaches that a marriage is not valid unless a couple are open to the possibility of having children. It does not, of course, suggest that a marriage without children is invalid since 10% of all couples are unable to conceive children. Other Christians, though, insist that the main purpose of being married is for the love between two people to grow and deepen. Although the vast majority of married couples do have children a marriage can still be a loving one without them.

Different terms

Three terms are used to describe the deliberate prevention of pregnancy:

1] Contraception Contraception is the deliberate avoidance of a pregnancy [contra-conception]. There are now various devices, and medications, available to make almost certain that pregnancy can be avoided.

2] Family planning Every couple can now decide whether they want children and, if they do, roughly when those children will be conceived. Various devices are available which mean that two people can have the size of family that they want. Unwanted children should now be a thing of the past.

3] Birth-control From time to time a country feels that it does not want its population to grow so quickly and it issues guidelines to prevent this. The various devices available can be used to limit the number of babies born in each family.

Methods of contraception

Until the 1930s the major Churches in Britain were against all forms of artificial contraception. During the Depression, though, the Church of England and the Nonconformist Churches became painfully aware of the link between the size of a family and poverty. Most Churches conceded that some form of 'birth prevention', as it was then called, was necessary. The Roman Catholic Church, however, has always remained implacably opposed to all forms of artificial birth-control although many individual Roman Catholics use them.

The main methods of contraception now available are:

1] The condom or sheath This is a tube of thin latex rubber which a man fits over his erect penis before any sexual contact takes place. The sheath then catches the man's sperm when he ejaculates. Used properly the sheath is a highly effective contraceptive as well as offering real protection against sexually transmitted diseases such as HIV.

2] The pill Over three million women in Britain, and 50 million worldwide, now use the

▶ Work to do

1 Write a sentence explaining the meaning of: a. Contraception.
b. Birth-control.
c. Family planning.

2 Write down TWO reasons why a couple might decide to use contraceptives.

3 Describe THREE methods of contraception.

4 Look at the quotations from the Bible in boxes 1 and 2. a. Do you think these two verses give someone the total freedom to have as many children as they want?
b. Do you think that all children are a gift from God.
c. Describe TWO situations in which a person might doubt that a child is a gift from God.

contraceptive pill. By altering the woman's hormonal cycle it renders her infertile making it impossible for her to conceive. The Pill is almost totally effective although some women suffer side-effects which make it dangerous for them to use it.

3] The IUD or coil
This is a small plastic device which is placed inside the woman's uterus and left there. It is only fitted in women who have already had a baby. It seems to work by bringing about a 'spontaneous abortion' [a miscarriage] if a fertilised egg imbeds itself in her uterine wall. Christians who feel strongly about abortion find the IUD morally unacceptable.

4] The diaphragm or cap A circular, rubber device which is fitted by the woman over the neck of her cervix before she has sex. This acts as a barrier against the man's sperm. It is left in place for several hours after intercourse.

5] Sterilisation In a woman the fallopian tubes which carry the egg to the uterus are cut. In a man the tubes which carry his sperm from the testicles to the penis are cut. In both men and women sterilisation leads to permanent infertility – although male sterilisation can be occasionally reversed. Sterilisation is particularly unacceptable to the Catholic Church since it means that sexual intercourse cannot lead to the creation of new life.

Many Christians regard sex as one of God's greatest gifts and so one to be enjoyed. For them contraception, in removing the fear of an unwanted pregnancy, is to be welcomed. Protestant Churches, including the Church of England, believe that any form of contraception is right as long as it is acceptable to both people. The Roman Catholic Church, though, is implacably opposed to all artificial ['unnatural] forms of contraception – as we shall see in unit 1.10.

[A] Why do you think that so many young women become pregnant when contraceptives are now so readily available?

1:10 | Contraception [2]

Roman Catholics believe that the love between a husband and a wife leads naturally to having children since children go to the very heart of that relationship. New life fulfils and completes married love. This is why the Catholic Church teaches that, in the words of Pope Paul VI: "…each and every marriage [sexual] act must remain open to the transmission of life." Married couples should see this as one of the most important aspects of their relationship. Their true vocation given to them by God is to create life. When they do so they are co-operating with their Creator and sharing in the fatherhood of God. At the same time, the Catholic Church recognises that many couples are, through no fault of their own, denied the God-given blessings of being parents. God, in his mercy, will compensate couples who are forced to pass through life childless.

KEY QUESTION

WHAT REASONS ARE GIVEN BY THE ROMAN CATHOLIC CHURCH FOR OPPOSING ALL FORMS OF ARTIFICIAL BIRTH-CONTROL?

BOX 1

HUMANAE VITAE

Condemned is any action, which either before, at the moment of, or after sexual intercourse is specifically intended to prevent procreation - whether as an end or a means - it is never lawful, even for the gravest of reasons, to do evil that good may come of it.

The regulation of birth

Until the 1930s all major Christian Churches were opposed to any attempt to regulate birth. The Lambeth Conference of the Anglican Church held just after the first World War said that all forms of contraception were morally and spiritually wrong. As we saw in unit 1.9 the Protestant Churches changed their minds during the 1920s and early 1930s when they saw the effect that too many children had on families struggling to fill empty stomachs.

Pope John XXIII [1958-63] set up a commission to look at the issue but it did not report until he had died. His successor, Pope Paul VI, was presented with two reports by the Commission:

1] A majority report which recommended that the Church should abandon its opposition to all means of artificial birth-control. It saw no compelling arguments against birth-control.

2] A minority report which urged the Pope to hold fast to the traditional teaching and rule out the use of artificial birth-control for all Catholics..

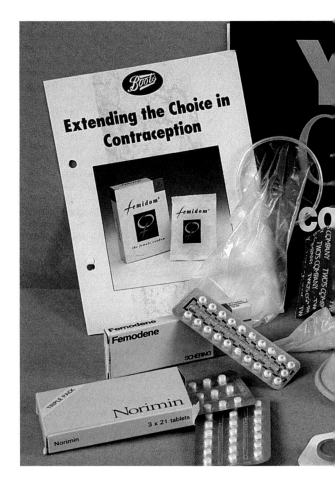

[A] What is the main difference between these contraceptives and Natural Family Planning

1 Pope Paul said: "Each and every married act must be open to the transmission of life…" Write TWO sentences describing what you think he meant by this.

2 a. What is Humanae Vitae?
b. What was the main teaching of Humanae Vitae and what reasons were given for its conclusions?
c. Why was Humanae Vitae, and its teaching, important for the Roman Catholic Church?

3 a. What do you think the Roman Catholic Church means when it says that every sexual act should be open to the transmission of new life?
b. What does the Roman Catholic Church mean when it says that it is against all 'unnatural' forms of birth-control?

Do you think that it is a misuse of sex to use it purely for pleasure - as the Roman Catholic Church suggests?

Pope Paul VI accepted the minority report. In 1968 the encyclical entitled 'Humanae Vitae' [On the Regulation of Life] was published outlawing the Pill and the condom together with sterilisation for all Roman Catholics. Only 'natural' forms of contraception were said to be in keeping with the purposes of God for marriage. Roman Catholics in the USA and Great Britain were deeply upset. Surveys suggest that as many as 80% of them ignored the Church's teaching on this matter at the time of the encyclical and continue to do so today.

Natural family planning

The reasons given by the Pope for opposing artificial means of contraception were:
a. The Church has always taught that it is wrong to interfere with the natural processes of conception and birth.
b. 'Natural Laws' exist which apply to all aspects of human behaviour. These 'laws' have been put in place by God as a way of bringing about maximum human happiness. If an activity is against God's natural laws it must be resisted. God intends that every sexual act must be open to the possibility of creating new life. It is immoral to interfere with this through unnatural forms of contraception.
c. Contraception is wrong because of the effect it has upon sexual intercourse. It turns an act designed to lead to the creation of new life into something that two people do purely for their own pleasure. Sexual intercourse should always strengthen the bond between husband and wife and the use of contraception cannot do this.
The Roman Catholic Church teaches that it is permissable for a couple to take advantage of those times in a month when a woman is infertile to limit the number of children that she conceives. These infertile days can be worked out by the woman taking her temperature carefully and measuring the consistency of the mucus in her cervix. Sexual intercourse can then be avoided on those days when these tests show that she is fertile.

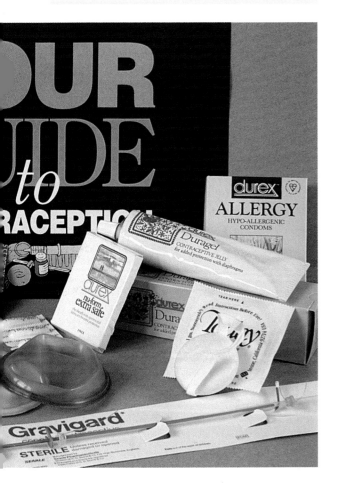

BOX 2

POPE JOHN PAUL II

Only natural forms of birth-control do not offend the moral order established by God.

23

1:11 Why Marry?

KEY QUESTION

WHY DO PEOPLE MARRY?

The number of first marriages in Britain has declined steadily since 1971. In that year 459,000 marriages took place of which almost 400,000 were first marriages. By 1997 this figure had dropped to 169,000. 50% of all marriages take place in a Register Office and most of the others in a place of worship, mainly a church. Whilst more than 50% of couples now live together before they marry 90% of women and 80% of men are married by the age of thirty. The average age at which people marry, though, is now about four years older than it was in 1970.

Why marry?

Although marriage is not as popular as it was it remains one of the most important institutions in society. Amongst the most important reasons for marriage are:

1] To make a public commitment to each other. A permanent relationship needs the help and support of other people. Marriage is not simply a private matter.

2] To have children and bring them up in a loving, secure and permanent relationship. Most people would want to be married if they have children – even if they happily co-habit before they start a family.

3] To channel the sexual drive and energy which are a basic part of a healthy relationship.

4] To develop a loving relationship which will grow through life.

The extract in box 1 provides an excellent summary of the reasons why the Christian Church supports marriage.

BOX 1

THE CHURCH OF ENGLAND. ALTERNATIVE SERVICE BOOK. 1980

It is God's purpose that as husband and wife give themselves to each other in love throughout their lives, they shall be united in that love as Christ is united with his Church. Marriage is given, that husband and wife may comfort and help each other, living faithfully together in need and plenty, in sorrow and in joy. It is given, that with delight and tenderness, they may know each other in love, and through the joy of their bodily union, may strengthen the union of their hearts and lives. It is given, that they may have children and be blessed in caring for them and bringing them up in accordance with God's will, to his praise and glory.

Marriage or living together?

1] FOR LIVING TOGETHER

a. Many people believe that living together is a good introduction to married life. They point out that by living together a couple can find out whether they are really suited to share the rest of their lives.

b. If they fall out of love then it is easier to break up a relationship if they are not married. Divorce is usually unpleasant and always expensive.

c. The couple may feel for unable to make a permanent commitment at the time but may still want to live together and share their lives.

2] AGAINST LIVING TOGETHER

a. Most Christians feel unhappy about two people living together without marrying. They feel that living together cannot be the same as marriage since it lacks the permanency and loyalty which marriage brings.

b. It is always better for children to be brought up in a stable relationship with two parents.

c. The clear teaching of Jesus was that marriage is the only place which express the full purpose that God has for two people who want to share their lives.

d. Within marriage the personal growth which everyone needs can take place.

e. Statistics show that marriages are more likely to break down if a couple has lived together before marrying.

1 Give THREE reasons why a couple might decide to marry.

2 Give TWO reasons why a couple might decide to live together rather than marry.

3 What do Christians understand to be the purpose of marriage?

4 Why might a Christian feel unhappy about living with a person without being married to them?

5 Read box 1 carefully. The wedding service in the Church of England give THREE reasons for marriage. What are they?

Mixed marriages

There are two kinds of 'mixed marriages' which are of concern here:

1] A marriage between two people, one of whom is a Christian and the other is not. The person who is not a Christian may not believe in God or may belong to another religious faith. One advantage of this kind of marriage is that the two people will bring to it the insights of their own religious culture and beliefs. To do this, of course, both of the people need to be open-minded enough to see that 'truth' does not come from just one direction. Unfortunately many religious people cannot do this. A religious commitment makes heavy demands on a person each week as well as at certain special times of the year – festivals etc. If one person is not a religious believer then he/she might find it difficult to understand these demands. Then there is the question of how any children should be brought up – should they be taken to church, taught to pray etc? These questions can easily divide believer and non-believer.

2] A marriage between Christians who come from different denominational backgrounds. If a Baptist marries a Catholic or a Pentecostalist marries an Orthodox Christian what problems might arise? There are still tensions amongst the different Churches although some of the barriers of ignorance and suspicion have been broken down in recent years. Problems might arise from the different approaches to worship. Can they sometimes worship together and, if not, does that matter? Are they happy to go in different directions each Sunday to church? Can they agree on how their children should be brought up – the Roman Catholic Church requires children in a mixed marriage to be brought up in the Catholic faith.

[A] This couple has been happily married for many years. What do you think might be the secret of a successful marriage?

1:12 | The Marriage Ceremony

KEY QUESTION

WHAT HAPPENS IN THE DIFFERENT CHRISTIAN MARRIAGE SERVICES?

About 50% of couples in this country are married in a religious ceremony in a church and about 50% go through a civil wedding ceremony. Most of the civil weddings are performed in a Register Office but, since 1997, other places such as stately homes and hotels have been able to apply for a licence to perform weddings.

There are several reasons why a couple might prefer a civil ceremony:

1] The couple do not feel happy taking vows in the presence of God when they are not Christian believers.

2] One, or both, of the partners is divorced and so cannot marry in a church. As more people divorce so the number of civil ceremonies is likely to increase - unless the Churches change their attitude towards the remarriage of divorced couples.

3] The couple do not want to promise that their relationship is permanent. Some couples feel uncomfortable about making this commitment and the civil ceremony does not require them to do so.

The Bible and marriage

Here are two quotations from the Bible which give a clear indication of its teaching about marriage:

1] The Lord God said, It is not good for man to be alone. I will make a helper fit for him... For this reason a man will leave his father and mother and be united to his wife, and they will become one flesh. *[Genesis 2.18,24]*.

2] That is why a man leaves his father and mother, and the two become one flesh. It follows that they are no longer two individuals: they are one flesh. Therefore what God has joined together, man must not separate. *[Matthew 19.4-6]*.

The Christian wedding service

Every Christian wedding service combines the legal and the religious. Although there are small variations between the various denominations they all follow a similar pattern:

1] The service stresses that the marriage is taking place 'in the sight of God' and in front of relatives and friends. Whilst there must be a minimum of two witnesses the most important witness of all to a Christian wedding is God. It is this, more than anything else, which marks the difference between a religious and a civil ceremony.

2] The marriage is intended to be a lifelong commitment between the two people. In all wedding services the couple promise that they will be faithful to each other 'until death us do part'.

3] The vows which the couple take [box 2] cover the whole area of human experience through which they are likely to pass - health and sickness, poverty and plenty. Through all of life's experiences the couple promise ' to love and cherish' one another till the end of their days. They promise to live together according to the principles that they find in the Bible and to solemnly promise to do so in the sight of God.

BOX 1

CHURCH OF ENGLAND. BOOK OF COMMON PRAYER

Dearly beloved, we are gathered together in the sight of God, and in the face of this congregation, to join together this man and this woman in holy matrimony.

BOX 2

THE VOWS

I, N take you, N, to be my husband/wife, to have and to hold from this day forward; for better, for worse, for richer, for poorer, in sickness and in health, to love and to cherish, till death us do part, according to God's holy law; and this is my solemn vow.

Talk it over

Some Christians believe that only practising Christians should be allowed to marry in a church - and make the vows. Do you agree? Give your reasons, one way or the other.

4] Rings are exchanged as a visible sign of the vows that they have taken [A]. The ring, a perfect and unending circle, symbolises that love which, it is hoped, will last and grow through life and into eternity.

There are two important denominational variations:

a. A wedding service involving two Roman Catholics ends with the celebration of a Nuptual Mass. In the Roman Catholic Church marriage is a sacrament but it is different from the other sacraments which the Church celebrates. Normally the sacrament is given by the priest to those participating but in the Nuptual Mass the couple give the sacrament, and its blessings, to each other.

b. In the Orthodox Church the service is called the 'crowning' during which crowns are placed on the heads of the bride and groom. The two of them both receive the power of the Holy Spirit to love each other, and any children that they might have. The crowns indicate both joy and self-sacrifice. For the marriage to be successful both must be present.

 Work to do

1. a. What is a civil marriage ceremony?
   b. What is a religious wedding ceremony?
   c. Give TWO reasons why a couple might prefer to have a civil rather than a religious wedding ceremony. d. What are TWO differences between a civil and a religious wedding ceremony?

2. Explain why a Christian couple would consider it important to marry in a religious rather than a civil wedding ceremony.

3. a. Put the marriage vows into your own words.
   b. Why do you think that the wedding vows are a very important part of the wedding ceremony.

[A] The giving, or exchanging of rings is an important part of a religious wedding ceremony. What do they symbolise?

BOX 3

CATHOLIC WEDDING SERVICE

May you always bear witness to the love of God in this world so that the afflicted and the needy will find in you generous friends, and welcome you into the joys of heaven.

1:13 | Divorce

KEY QUESTION

WHAT IS THE LAW ABOUT DIVORCE AND WHAT IS THE CHRISTIAN ATTITUDE TOWARDS IT?

It is commonly argued that more marriages are likely to end in divorce and so the idea of marriage for life is becoming increasingly unrealistic. It is true that the number of divorces in the United Kingdom has increased from 26,000 a year in 1960 to over 170,000 today. Today 1 in 4 of every new marriages will end in divorce. At the same time the number of people remarrying has remained constant, at around 125,000, since 1971. The interesting thing is that the trauma of divorce does not seem to put most people off marriage. The vast majority remarry.

Divorce and the Law

In 1857 the Matrimonial Causes Act made it possible, for the first time, for both men and women to divorce. However, whilst a man could divorce his wife on the ground of adultery alone a wife had to prove adultery and cruelty. It was not until 1923 that the two sexes were given equal rights. After 1923 custody of any children usually went to the woman. Then, in 1937, desertion, cruelty and insanity were added to adultery as grounds for divorce. The Divorce Reform Act of 1969 allowed divorce if a marriage had 'irretrievably broken down'. Adultery, cruelty or desertion could be used to prove that this had happened. If both people agreed on the divorce then a two year separation period was necessary but if only one person wanted the divorce then a five year separation was required. After 1996 divorce became possible after a one year separation.

[A] Do you think more preparation before marriage would help to cut down on the divorce rate?

BOX 1

MARK 10.11,12

Anyone who divorces his wife and marries another woman commits adultery against her. And if she divorces her husband and marries another man, she commits adultery.

Talk it over

Do you think it is too easy to get a divorce in Great Britain? If you had your way what would the law on divorce be?

 Work to do

1 State TWO reasons why many Christians believe that divorce is wrong.

2 The remarriage of divorced persons is allowed in some churches. Give ONE reason for this.

3 State TWO ways in which a divorce might affect family life.

4 What did Jesus teach about divorce?

5 Describe and explain the current divorce laws in Britain.

6 Why do marriages break up?

Who wins?

Divorce may now be easier but it remains a very painful business for everyone involved. Couples often experience a sense of failure at the break-up of their relationship. One or both partners may have to face the future alone - often with dependent children to look after. There are about 1,300,000 single-parent families in Great Britain and the majority of these are created by divorce [see unit 1.8]. In 1998 7% of all families were of a single-parent with dependent children and these families were amongst the poorest in the country. 70% of all divorcing couples have children and 75% of these are under the age of 16. There are 1,600,000 children under the age of 16 who are the victims of the divorce of their parents. Before granting a divorce a judge must be satisfied that satisfactory arrangements have been made for any dependent children.

Christians and divorce

Jesus often reminded his listeners about the purpose of marriage and the sort of relationship that God had intended it to be. Moses, the great Jewish law-giver, had allowed divorce because the people failed to live up to God's ideal for marriage. Yet that was always a compromise and not part of God's original plan [box 2]. Jesus seems to have ruled out divorce altogether. Anyone who leaves

---

BOX 2

MATTHEW 19.5-6

Haven't you read... that at the beginning the Creator made them male and female and said 'For this reason a man will leave his father and mother and be united with his wife, and the two will become one flesh. So they are no longer two, but one. Therefore what God has joined together, let man not separate...'

---

their wife and marries someone else, he said, commits adultery [box 1] and that was forbidden in the Ten Commandments *[Exodus 20.14]*. It is a little strange to read, in box 1, of a woman leaving her husband and marrying someone else since Jewish women had no right to divorce in 1st century Palestine. Divorce was only available to men.

The attitudes of the different Churches towards divorce today differs:

1] The Church of England accepts divorce as a social necessity but will not remarry divorced people. Instead, it encourages couples to marry in a civil ceremony and then to go to church afterwards to receive a blessing from the priest.

2] The Roman Catholic Church believes that marriage is a sacrament and so cannot be dissolved. Instead, it encourages those whose marriage has broken down to either separate from their partner but remain married or seek an annulment. After an annulment it is as if the marriage has never taken place. An annulment can be granted if it can be shown that the couple did not fully understand what they were doing when they married; one of the people did not give their full consent to the marriage or if one of the partners did not intend to have children at any time.

3] Nonconformist Churches allow divorced people to remarry in church although individual ministers can refuse to perform the ceremony if it is in conflict with their own beliefs about marriage.

BOX 3

1 CORINTHIANS 7.10,11

A wife must not separate from her husband. But if she does, she must remain unmarried or else be reconciled to her husband. And a husband must not divorce his wife.

Leviticus 18.22; Romans 1.26,27; 1.Corinthians 6.9.

1:14 Homosexuality

KEY QUESTION

WHAT IS HOMOSEXUALITY AND WHAT IS THE CHRISTIAN ATTITUDE TOWARDS IT?

Homosexuality, from the Latin word meaning 'same', refers to sexual orientation and relationships between members of the same sex, male or female. Although homosexuality stretches back at least as far as the ancient Greeks the word itself was only coined in 1869. The word 'lesbian' was also brought into use about the same time to describe female homosexuals. This word was taken from the name of the Greek island of Lesbos where, in the 7th century BCE, the Greek poetess Sappho formed an all-female community of followers.

Homosexuals and the law

In recent years most male homosexuals have preferred to call themselves 'gay'. No-one knows just how many gay people there are in this country. It is thought that about 1 in every 15 people is gay or lesbian - 60% of them men and 40% women. Of this number only about 10% are openly gay - the remainder preferring to keep their sexual orientation secret.

Until 1967 it was illegal for any man to be involved in homosexual activity. No law has ever been passed in this country against female homosexual activity, largely because law-makers early in the 20th century found it impossible to believe that any women would be involved in such an activity. In 1967 the law was changed to make homosexual activity amongst men legal as long as:

1] All such activity was carried out in private.

2] Those involved were consenting adults, aged 21 and over. This age-limit was later lowered to 18 and moves were afoot in 2000 to reduce it still further to 16. This would be important symbolically since the age for lawful sexual intercourse in this country would then be the same for homosexuals and heterosexuals.

BOX 1

ROMANS 1.26,27

God gave them over to shameful lusts. Even their women exchanged natural relations for unnatural ones. In the same way the men also abandoned natural relations with women and were inflamed with lust for one another. Men committed indecent acts with other men...

Why are some people homosexual?

There is no certain answer but several explanations have been put forward:

1] Some people are born homosexual. As it is part of their genetic make-up there is nothing they can do about it. Our heterosexual or homosexual orientation is genetically determined.

2] Family background or circumstances explain it. It has been suggested, for instance, that boys who have very strong emotional links with their mothers, and weak links with their fathers, are more likely to be homosexual.

3] It is pure accident whether we are homosexual or heterosexual. Childhood influences and teenage sexual experiences determine which of the two life-styles we end up adopting.

Christianity and homosexuality

Homosexuality was one of the most hotly debated issues in the Christian Church as it approached the third millennium. Many Christians believe that the Bible condemns homosexuality without reservation. If a person is homosexual, and many Christians are, then they must accept it and not take part in any homosexual activities. This was the

BOX 2

METHODIST CHURCH REPORT. 1979

For homosexual men and women permanent relationships characterised by love can be appropriate and the Christian way of expressing their sexuality

conclusion of a debate held in the General Synod of the Church of England in 1987 - no-one can be blamed for their sexual orientation but it is quite wrong for them to take part in any homosexual activity.

Without any doubt many Christian priests are homosexual - one estimate puts the figure at 1 in 4 of all Church of England priests. The official line of the Church of England is to be less tolerant of homosexuality amongst the clergy than it is among ordinary church members. On this issue, however, the Methodist Church has a history of following a more tolerant line than other Churches. A Methodist report issued in 1979 [box 2] argued that the Church should recognise that many gay people are in meaningful relationships which the Church should do everything in its power to support and not destroy.

 Talk it over

In a survey conducted in 1992 almost 80% of people interviewed believed that the law should treat homosexuals and heterosexuals in exactly the same way. Do you agree with this?

[A] How would you describe the attitude of society as a whole towards homosexuality at the start of a new millennium?

 Work to do

1 Describe the meaning of these three words:
a. Homosexuality.
b. Lesbian.
c. Gay.

2 What explanations have been put forward to explain why some people are homosexual and others are not.

3 What are the different Christian attitudes towards homosexuality?

4 Do you think that the Church has got it about right in the way that it treats homosexuals - or do you think that some changes need to be made?

1:15 | Aids and HIV

KEY QUESTION

WHAT IS THE AIDS EPIDEMIC?

AIDS is caused by a virus - the Human Immuno-Deficiency Virus [HIV]. If the virus enters the bloodstream it attacks the cells which maintain the body's natural defence mechanisms. Once inside a cell the virus multiplies until it eventually destroys the cell. The body's natural mechanisms are damaged so that the person is unable to recover from a wide variety of illnesses. No-one knows why the HIV virus suddenly becomes active after lying dormant for years in the body. Current treatments available, though, delay the transition from HIV to AIDS so prolonging the active life of sufferers by many years.

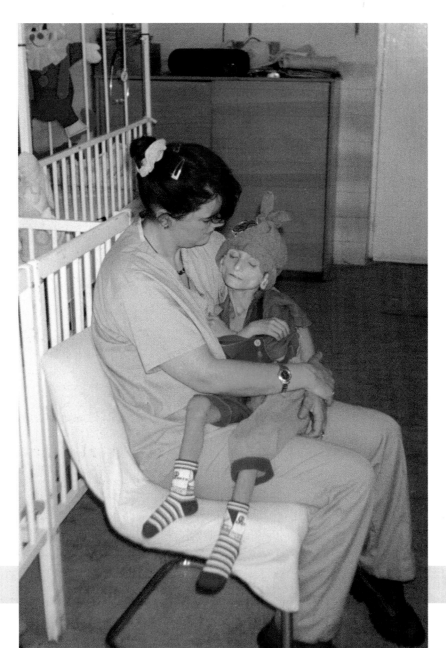

[A] This is a AIDS hospice in Rumania which looks after children with the disease. How could a young children be born infected with the virus?

Catching HIV

The number of people catching HIV in the United Kingdom continues to increase. In 1997 2,615 new cases were reported although the number going on to develop AIDS, 1,171, was the lowest for over a decade. The number of people dying from AIDS related illnesses at 654 was also the lowest for some years. About 70% of those contracting HIV were homosexual and 30% heterosexual. Worldwide, especially in African countries, the situation is much more serious with over 34 million people thought to have AIDS by the end of 1999. It is estimated that more people will die of AIDS related illnesses in the world between

Some people have said that the only way to stop the spread of AIDS is to go back to the old Christian virtues of chastity outside marriage and faithfulness within it. Do you think it really could be that simple?

1 a. What is HIV?
  b. What is AIDS?
  c. Why is there now more hope for people who have the HIV virus?

2 Explain how the HIV virus is caught and what can be done to protect oneself against it?

3 How has society, and many Christians, dealt with the AIDS crisis?

4 a. What is homophobia?
  b. Do you think that some people, especially in the early days, used the AIDS crisis to reinforce their own homophobia?

2000 and 2010 than died from war in the whole of the 20th century - over 100 million people. Virtually all of those in Africa with AIDS were infected through unprotected sexual intercourse between men and women. Homosexuality is almost unknown in Africa.

There are two main ways in which the HIV virus is passed from one person to another:

1] **Unprotected anal intercourse** This takes place when the penis enters the anus, or back passage and is very risky since the skin in the anus is particularly fragile. This is the main way that the virus is transferred during homosexual activity.

2] **Unprotected vaginal intercourse** The virus can be passed on by both men and women in this way through semen or vaginal juices.

There is also a much smaller risk when oral sex takes place. This is when a person stimulates the sexual organs of another person with their tongue. Using a condom properly is the only effective safeguard against being infected with the HIV virus.

Many questions

When news about AIDS first reached this country in the early 1980s it was greeted with panic. Labelled 'the gay plague' by tabloid newspapers it was thought that only homosexuals could catch it –

BOX 1

GOVERNMENT LEAFLET
SENT TO EVERY HOME. 1987

Any man or woman can get the AIDS virus depending on their behaviour. It is not just a homosexual disease. There is no cure and it kills. By the time you have read this probably 300 people will have died in this country from the virus. It is believed a further 30,000 people carry the virus. The number is rising and will continue to rise unless we all take precautions.

---

and this led to an outbreak of 'homophobia' i.e. an irrational fear of homosexuality. Many spoke of it as the judgement of God upon homosexuals whilst others called the virus the modern equivalent of the biblical disease of leprosy.

Twenty years later AIDS is forcing people, and especially Christians, to ask many awkward questions about themselves and their attitudes to others. For instance:

1] What kind of practical help can be given to those with AIDS - and the people who care for them? As you can see from A many of the sufferers worldwide are children who are born to mothers who have the virus.

2] What is the attitude of heterosexual people towards the gay community? Many gay relationships have borne the brunt of the disease and yet society gives them very little support. A recent survey of homosexuals found that 48% of them had been insulted at work because of their life-style.

3] Should pregnant women with HIV be given the opportunity to abort their unborn child? There is a very real risk that an infected mother will pass that infection on to the unborn - who will almost certainly die before reaching its 10th birthday

4] Are we doing enough to educate young and old about the dangers of catching AIDS? The 1995 Health Education Monitoring Survey found that around 15% of those surveyed between the ages of 16 and 24 thought that there was no chance of 'someone like me getting the HIV or AIDS virus'. Over 40% of those surveyed between 45 and 55 thought this way.

2:1 | The Law - and Breaking It

Criminal activity, the breaking of the law, both fascinates and disturbs. It fascinates, as numerous television programmes demonstrate, since criminal behaviour is out of the ordinary – and exciting. We find the constant battle between good and evil fascinating. It disturbs us because criminal activity frightens – and occasionally involves us as its victims.

[A] Bye-laws often matter more to people than national laws. Why do you think this is?

The law

There are two kinds of laws in Britain:
1] BYE-LAWS These are laws which only relate to a local area. Bye-laws are made by the local council. These laws have the power, for example, to determine where we take or park our car, where we do and do not walk etc. They also determine what penalties will be paid by those who break the law. Often punishment is by a fixed fine which offenders are given the opportunity of paying without going to court. If we break one of these laws we do not have a criminal record. It is dealt with quickly, without fuss, and then forgotten.
2] PARLIAMENTARY LAWS Bye-laws only apply locally but the laws passed by Parliament apply nationally. Some of the laws on the statute-book go back into the 19th century, or beyond, although sometimes they are updated to take modern conditions into account. From time to time the law on a particular issue is changed. Two good examples of this are:

a. The law on homosexuality. Prior to 1967 all homosexual activity between men was illegal but, in that year, it became legal as long as it involved men aged 21 and over and was conducted in private. Later the age limit was lowered to 18 and in the year 2000 moves were afoot to reduce it still further to 16. See unit 1.14 for more information.

b. In 1967 also the law was changed to allow abortion under certain strict conditions whereas previously it had been illegal. See units 2.24 and 2.25 for more information about abortion.

Clearly the law does not stand still. It changes as society changes. Sometimes practices which were abhorrent to previous generations become acceptable and the law is changed to take this into account.

Breaking the law

Criminal offences are divided into two categories:
1] Non-indictable offences These cover minor offences such as petty theft and less serious motoring offences. Non-indictable offences are dealt with in a magistrate's court.
2] Indictable offences These are the most serious crimes such as murder, manslaughter and rape. Usually these crimes are dealt with by a judge, often sitting with a jury.

No Parking

Motorists failing to comply with parking restrictions on Railway property are liable to prosecution under Byelaw 25

[B] To what extent do you think the explosion in car ownership has affected the number of crimes committed?

The number of crimes reported to the police in 1997 was 4.6 million. This was the first time that the number had fallen below 5 million since 1990. In this number:
• 6% of households [about 1 in every 16] were burgled.
• 508,00 people were found guilty of committing an offence or were cautioned by the police.
• 28% of all recorded crime was cleared up [called the 'detection rate']. This compares with 38% in 1981.
• Men were seven times more likely to commit a crime than women.
• The age-group responsible for the highest number of crimes was 16–24 year olds.

Many reasons have been put forward to explain the rise in crime since 1951 when there were 638,000 reported offences. Some of these reasons are purely practical reflecting changes in everyday life - there is so much more to steal now, few people owned a car in the 1950s, everyone now has a phone to report crime etc. Other questions, though, about criminal activity have wider implications. Does the increase in criminal activity show a breakdown in moral and religious values in society? How much is unemployment, especially amongst young people, responsible for the great increase in drug-taking and vandalism? Does advertising and television stimulate greed and the desire to possess what we cannot afford. Only 1 in 4 crimes leads to a conviction - perhaps a higher clear-up rate would act as a deterrent? Is there any truth in the old belief that human nature is naturally sinful and crime is just one expression of this?

 Work to do

1 What is:
a. A bye-law.
b. A Parliamentary law?
What is the difference between the two?

2 Outline two examples of the law being changed in recent years to bring it more into line with public opinion.

3 What are:
a. Non-indictable offences?
b. Indictable offences ?

4 What reasons have been put forward to explain the large increase that there has been in law-breaking in the last 50 years?

BOX 1

DAVID MACLEAN, HOME OFFICE MINISTER 1994

The recent drop in crime shows that it is not bound irremediably and irrevocably to rise. By targeting and crime prevention campaigns, we can make a difference. The message has to be that the fear of crime must now reduce. The fear of crime in many people is worse than the problem itself.

2:2 Punishment

KEY QUESTION

WHAT SHOULD ALL FORMS OF PUNISHMENT SET OUT TO ACHIEVE?

Punishment is the way in which society makes people 'pay' for any criminal activity. The payment may involve a loss of their freedom [prison]; the inconvenience of having their freedom restricted [probation or tagging] or the payment of a sum of money [a fine]. All punishment sets out to achieve, to a greater or lesser extent, five objectives:

1] RETRIBUTION This is quite simply making a person pay for the wrong that they have done. The criminal is believed to owe society a debt - the more serious the crime, the greater the debt. The problem is deciding what punishment is appropriate for the crime that has been committed. This becomes particularly difficult when we look at Capital Punishment [unit 2.3]. Almost every country in Europe, for instance, has abandoned capital punishment [killing the criminal] as an appropriate way of dealing with even the most serious of crimes. In the USA, however, the death penalty remains in most States and the number of people being put to death for their crimes is increasing year by year. The same is true in almost eighty other countries.

2] DETERRENCE Punishment is intended to deter the person who committed the crime from carrying out a similar act in future. It is also intended to remind other people what punishment they can expect to receive if they commit a similar offence. Opinion is sharply divided, however, as to how effective punishment is as a deterrent. 75% of all criminals are recidivists i.e. they offend again. The number of murders committed in the USA has continued to rise since the Death Penalty was re-introduced and stepped up in 1976.

3] PROTECTION Criminals threaten the stability of society. Most people would agree that society needs to take all the protective measures it can against them. Two such measures have been introduced in recent years - the widespread use of closed circuit television in vulnerable areas and the use of 'tagging' to keep track of criminals released early from prison. Locking a prisoner away at least guarantees the safety of society whilst that person is in prison. Most people would see this as the main reason for a prison sentence.

4] REFORMATION Whilst a person is in prison it is important that every attempt should be made to reform him or her - to change their ways. Over 200,000 young offenders pass through the juvenile courts each year and these are people in danger of embarking on a life of crime. It is obviously in everyone's interests if every attempt is made to change their ways before they become habitual criminals. In some prisons attempts are made to teach prisoners, give them a trade, find them somewhere to live when they leave prison and arrange a

BOX 1

LEVITICUS 24. 17-19

If anyone takes the life of a human being, he must be put to death. Anyone who takes the life of someone's animal must make restitution - life for life. If anyone injures his neighbour, whatever he has done must be done to him: fracture for fracture, eye for eye, tooth for tooth. As he has injured the other so he must be injured... I am the Lord your God.

Talk it over

One of the main purposes of punishment is to deter a person from committing the crime again - and to put others off as well. Do you think this is likely to happen or are there stronger forces which lead a person into criminal activity?

job for them. At the same time sessions are held to encourage them to see the consequences of the criminal way of life that they are following and the effect that their crimes have upon their victims. This is very important reformative work. Prisons, though, are severely overcrowded with around 67,000 people in 1997 occupying space, and facilities, designed for less than 30,000. This makes it very difficult to carry out effective reformative work.

5] COMPENSATION Everything so far has concentrated on the needs of the prisoner. In all crime, however, there is a victim and he or she is too easily forgotten. Victims can receive money compensation for suffering and loss suffered at the hands of a criminal. More important, however, are recent attempts to make criminals face up to the consequences of their criminal actions. Sometimes the victim and the criminal are brought face to face. This often has an enormous effect on the criminal as well as helping the victim to forgive – if not to forget.

The Bible and punishment

The Old Testament emphasises that the criminal should be punished for his or her crime. Known as the law of 'lex talionis' it was very simply stated as exacting the very same suffering as the criminal inflicted on the victim [box 1]. This was the law at the time of Jesus but he tried to steer his listeners towards a more compassionate understanding of punishment. He encouraged his followers not to judge other people in case the same standard of judgement was applied to them [Matthew 7.1]. When Jesus was dying on the cross for a crime that he did not commit he asked his followers to forgive those who were responsible for this crime [Luke 12.34]. The need to forgive those who have wronged us is a whole new area of Christian responsibility and we will look at this in unit 2.4.

BOX 2

MATTHEW 7.1

Do not judge, or you too will be judged. For in the same way as you judge others, you will be judged…

[A] The outside of a prison. Do you think that prisons are an effective way of punishing people today or should other ways of punishment be sought?

Work to do

1 Describe TWO aims of all punishment.

2 Many Christians believe that the emphasis today should be on reforming the criminal rather than trying to punish him or her. Do you agree with this point of view?

3 Why do people think that it is important for offenders to be punished in an appropriate way?

4 Place the five purposes of punishment in what you consider to be the order of importance. Give THREE reasons for the order that you have given.

2:3 | Capital Punishment

WHAT IS CAPITAL PUNISHMENT AND WHY ARE MANY CHRISTIANS OPPOSED TO IT?

Putting someone to death for committing murder is not a new idea. In the Old Testament the punishment for a crime was exactly the same as the crime itself – including murder. The Romans crucified all non-Roman criminals and beheaded Romans who committed serious crimes. In 18th century Britain there were over 200 offences for which a person could be hanged.

In 1957 Capital Punishment was restricted in this country to the crimes of:
1] Killing a policeman.
2] Killing whilst carrying out an armed robbery.
3] Killing by explosion.
4] Killing more than one person at the same time.

In 1965 Parliament suspended the use of the Death Penalty for a trial period of five years and in 1970 it was abolished altogether. Gradually most of the countries in Europe followed suit and it became a condition for membership of the European Community. In December 1999, for instance, Turkey was invited to apply for membership and one of the conditions laid down was that the Death Penalty must be abolished in that country. It still remains, though, in 78 countries which, in 1998, had 3,899 criminals under sentence of death. In 1998 1,625 executions were carried out in 37 different countries. Over 1,000 people were executed in China in alone. Hundreds were put to death in Iraq, Congo and the USA.

For and against the Death Penalty

Clearly the debate about Capital Punishment, whilst largely over in the United Kingdom, is still a live issue in many other countries. The arguments for and against it can be marshalled as follows:
1] FOR THE DEATH PENALTY
a. The Death Penalty is a proper form of retribution - the most appropriate penalty for those who take the life of someone else. Retribution, as we saw in unit 2.2, is a proper element in all punishment.
b. Some people in our society only understand the language of violence. Capital Punishment is the only effective deterrent for naturally violent people. Violent people only understand, and respect, a violent response from society to their criminal activity.
c. Putting a murderer to death is the only effective way of protecting society - otherwise the murderer is able to murder again. Protecting society is a very important purpose of punishment.
d. Society has a duty to protect its most vulnerable members. The group most at risk in society from violence are children under the age of one. Society must also protect those in the frontline of the battle against crime - police officers, prison warders etc. Only Capital Punishment is able to offer this protection.
e. A 'life sentence' does not mean life these days, except in the most extreme cases. When a prisoner is released he or she is free to murder again.
2] AGAINST THE DEATH PENALTY
a. Only God has the right to give, and take away, human life. The justice system is not infallible and mistakes can be made. We know that more than one innocent person was executed in Britain before Capital Punishment was abolished.
b. There is no conclusive evidence that the Death Penalty is an effective deterrent. In New York, for instance, where the Death Penalty operates the murder rate is 14 times higher than it is in the UK and going up year by year.
c. Executing people who kill for political reasons such as terrorists simply makes them martyrs, which in turn leads to more deaths.

? **Find out**

Find out as much as you can about the
work of Amnesty International.

[A] Why do you think that
most people in Great
Britain are in favour of the
death penalty?

d. The Death Penalty is barbaric. It barbarises
those who prepare a person for execution and it
does the same to those who carry out the death
sentence.

'Amnesty International'

Amnesty International is an organisation which is
in the forefront of those which seek the universal
abolition of the Death Penalty. Countries, such as
China which executes far more people than any
other country, tries to keep such executions as
quiet as possible. Amnesty International compiles
statistics of people executed throughout the world
and publishes them. It also hires lawyers to defend
people who are on trial for their lives.

 Work to do

1 a. What is Capital Punishment?
b. Why do you think that many
Christians support the use of Capital
Punishment?
c. Explain why you think that many
Christians are against Capital Punishment.

2 "Christians could never agree with the
use of Capital Punishment." Do you
agree?

3 a. State TWO reasons why a Christian
might support the reintroduction of the
Death Penalty in this country.
b. State TWO reasons why a Christian might
oppose the reintroduction of the Death
Penalty.

BOX 1
AMNESTY INTERNATIONAL
Capital Punishment is the ultimate cruel, inhuman and degrading punishment which violates every person's right to life.

2:4 Forgiveness

In approaching the issue of punishment Christians try to find a middle line between the demands of justice and the need for mercy and forgiveness. Christians can never agree with an approach to punishment which says 'Lock the door and throw away the key.' They believe that it should be possible for everyone to find forgiveness – from God and from society – whatever they have done.

The Unmerciful Servant

Jesus introduced a new strain of thinking about punishment and the need to show mercy. In the Beatitudes - eight sayings which sum up his whole teaching - Jesus said: "Blessed are the merciful, for they will be shown mercy." *[Matthew 5.7]*. The need to show mercy to others was highlighted in the parable that Jesus told about the unmerciful servant *[Matthew 18. 21-35]*. A servant who owed his master a large sum of money is called to account but, after begging for mercy, has his debt cancelled. The same servant then goes out and finds someone who owes him much less money. Rather than cancel the debt he has the man thrown into prison. When he hears of this his master reinstates the man's debt and has him thrown into prison to be tortured. Jesus used the parable to remind his followers of the debt they owed God. If God can forgive their debts they can forgive everyone else - no matter what they have done.

Forgiveness

Jesus had more to say about forgiveness than almost anything else in his ministry. He reminded his listeners that God was ready to forgive anyone who repented of their sins and sought his forgiveness. This theme runs through the whole of the New Testament. Here are some examples:

1] The three parables in Luke 15 - the lost sheep, the lost coin and the lost son - each have the same theme. There is great joy when the coin and the sheep are found and when the son returns to his father. In the most important of these parables, the lost son *[vs 11-32]*, Jesus wanted his followers to see God as the father in the story and each human being as the son. The father watches for a long time waiting for the son to return and, when he sees his son in the distance, runs to him and throws his arms around the boy's neck. Similarly God is desperate to offer his forgiveness to all those who return to him

2] Forgiveness is a two-way business. In the Lord's Prayer Jesus included the phrase: "Forgive us our debts as we also have forgiven our debtors". *[Matthew 6.12]*. He adds: "For if you forgive men when they sin against you, your heavenly Father will also forgive you. But if you do not forgive men their sins, your Father will not forgive your sins." *[Matthew 6.14,15]*. These words of Jesus would seem to apply, amongst other situations, to the relationship between the criminal and the victim. It seems almost impossible to forgive a serious crime - such as rape or grievous bodily harm. Yet Jesus implies that we are all in need of

BOX 1

MATTHEW 18. 21,22

Then Peter came to Jesus and asked, "Lord, how many times shall I forgive my brother when he sins against me? Up to seven times? Jesus answered,"I tell you, not seven times but seventy seven times.

BOX 2

ROMANS 12.17-21

Do not repay anyone evil for evil. Be careful to do what is right in the eyes of everybody. If it is possible, as far as it depends on you, live at peace with everyone. Do not take revenge, my friends, but leave room for God's wrath, for it is written: 'It is mine to avenge; I will repay,' says the Lord. On the contrary:'If your enemy is hungry feed him; if he is thirsty, give him something to drink…Do not be overcome by evil, but overcome evil with good.

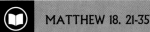
1 Jesus taught that all his followers should be ready to forgive others. a. Describe ONE incident in the life of Jesus when he showed what forgiveness really meant.
b. Describe ONE parable told by Jesus in which he explained what forgiveness really means.

2 What did Jesus teach about forgiveness in the Sermon on the Mount in Matthew 5-7? Do you think that it is practical for Christians to follow the teaching of Jesus on this?

3 "Forgive us our debts as we forgive our debtors." Do you think that these words of Jesus should influence our attitude towards anyone who commits a criminal act against us? Explain your reasons, either way.

4 Sum up TWO things that the quotation in box 2 says about forgiveness.

God's forgiveness – and that this forgiveness depends on our ability to forgive other people [box 1]

3] Jesus always showed God's forgiveness but at no time was this shown more clearly than at the end of his life. Crucified between two thieves Luke tells us that one of the criminals turned to Jesus asking for his forgiveness [Luke 23. 39-43]. He received it and Jesus promised him that the two of them would be reunited in paradise.

4] Paul underlined that revenge is not a Christian emotion although it may be the natural response when one is hurt or injured. In his letter to the Romans [see box 2] he attacked the idea that Christians should return evil for evil. Revenge can safely be left to God to carry out in his own good time. Christians should respond to evil by feeding, and giving water, to their enemy so that good can finally overcome evil.

Forgiveness is probably the hardest demand that Jesus makes on all his followers – but there is no limit to the forgiveness that God expects them to show. For those who have been hurt and bruised through the criminal behaviour of others this is very hard. Some would even say that it is asking the impossible.

[A] For which groups of people does this candle encourage Christians to pray for - and why?

THIS CANDLE BURNS CONTINUOUSLY FOR THE RELEASE OF ALL PRISONERS OF INJUSTICE, FOR THEIR CAPTORS, AND FOR PEACE IN THE WORLD.

2:5 | Drugs [1]

A drug is any substance which has a chemical effect on the body when it is injected, swallowed, smoked or inhaled. Some drugs affect the delicate balance that exists between mind and body so that they have mental, emotional and psychological as well as physical effects.

A social problem

Illegal drug-taking in Great Britain creates enormous social as well as personal problems. Consider the following:

1] The number of people convicted of drug offences in Great Britain went up by 400% between 1987 and 1997. In 1997 the number of people cautioned or convicted of drug offences was 113,200 compared with 26,000 ten years earlier. Over 14,000 of these people were convicted of dealing in drugs. Surveys suggest that almost 50% of young people use drugs at some time - the majority using cannabis.

2] Drug users are now responsible for 30% of all theft, robberies and burglaries in the country. Serious drug users commonly spend between £300 and £2000 a week on their habit and nearly all of this is raised illegally. Users acquire £850 million a year through crime but the cost to the victims is over £2.5 billion. In this way drug-taking involves everyone in society.

3] 51% of male prisoners on remand in prison and awaiting trial have some history of drug dependence.

Drugs - why take them?

There may be many reasons why a person starts using drugs. Amongst the reasons are likely to be:

1] The pressure of their peer group. The vast majority of people who take drugs begin when they are young and they are most likely to be introduced to them through their friends. This is the age when the pressure from the peer group is greatest and most difficult to resist.

2] Boredom

3] Anxiety and tension

4] Personal problems - with parents or work at school. Drug-taking is also common amongst people in their twenties who are in very high powered jobs.

5] Experimentation. Drugs have a novelty interest for people who haven't taken them before.

6] Rebellion - against parents, society etc.

 Talk it over

Do you think that education about drug-taking, and its effects, is the most effective way of persuading young people to give it a miss? Do you think that young people are given enough information about drug-taking?

 Work to do

1 What are the main reasons for people taking drugs?

2 a. What are the main kinds of drugs available today?
b. How do drugs affect the body?
c. What kinds of pressures might lead a person to start taking drugs?

3 Describe THREE of the non-physical consequences that might affect a person as a result of taking drugs.

4 What are the main effects of taking drugs?

[A] Why could drug taking be described as a 'Catch 22' situation?

The effects

The actual effect that a chemical substance has upon the body varies from substance to substance. Drugs can cause:

1] Depression and sleep problems. Drugs often give a momentary boost to the person taking them before plunging them into a deep emotional depression.

2] Rapid mood swings.

3] Restlessness, sweating, panic and anxiety attacks.

4] Drowsiness and a feeling similar to drunkeness.

5] Confusion and hallucinations

6] Chronic constipation and a disruption of the menstrual cycle.

7] Mental imbalance

8] HIV

9] Permanent injury to the liver, kidneys and heart. In some situations, such as the mixing of drugs and alcohol, the outcome can be disastrous, even death.

Drug-taking places an enormous strain on all personal relationships - with parents, friends, husband or wife, employer, work-mates etc. As an extremely expensive habit drug-taking is likely to lead to severe money problems. Drug-taking is a 'Catch 22' situation - the habit is frightenly expensive but taking drugs makes it increasingly difficult to hold down any form of regular employment. The link between drug-taking and crime means that a person can easily acquire a police record through their habit - with all the consequences that this will have for future job prospects.

 Find out

Find out the main drugs which are taken illegally today - how they are taken; what they do to the person who takes them and what risks are involved in taking them.

2:6 Drugs [2]

KEY QUESTION

WHAT IS DRUG ADDICTION AND HOW CAN A PERSON BE HELPED TO OVERCOME IT?

In unit 2.5 we saw how illegal drug-taking can have a devastating effect on both an individual and the people around them. We also saw how a whole range of social problems - including crime, divorce, homelessness and premature death - often have a close link with illegal drug consumption. Here we look at the way back that people who are seriously addicted to drugs have to tread if they wish to have any kind of hopeful future.

Drug abuse

Millions of drugs are prescribed each year by doctors for their patients. The prescribing and the taking of these drugs are carefully controlled and so little abuse of them takes place. Some tablets taken, though, to help people relax such as sleeping pills and relaxants can lead to a form of addiction of their own. Almost 5 million sleeping tablets are taken each night in this country, for example, and it is thought that 500,000 people are addicted or dependent on them. Nearly all of these are elderly people.

[A] How do you think that professional counselling might help some people who abuse drugs?

Talk it over

**Do you think that work amongst
drug addicts is an activity in which
Christians should be heavily involved?
Give your reasons, either way.**

Obviously, it is much easier for a person to abuse their bodies and become drug dependent/addicted if they take substances illegally. Dependency, which is one step away from addiction, can take one of two forms although in the most seriously affected both are involved:

1] PSYCHOLOGICAL DEPENDENCY This happens when a person begins to 'feel' that they cannot cope without taking the drug. For example, someone who is prescribed a sleeping pill may be initially grateful that they can get a good night's sleep. Before long, however, that person may become convinced that they can never have a good night's sleep without a pill. That is psychological dependence. For the illegal drug-taker such psychological dependence works hands in hand with a physical dependency. They begin to feel that they could not manage without the physical effects brought on by the drug - liveliness, talkativeness, energy, alertness etc

2] A PHYSICAL DEPENDENCE After some time, people who take a drug will feel that their body needs it more and more. If they are deprived of the drug for any length of time they suffer highly unpleasant withdrawal symptoms. These symptoms only stop when they take more of the drug. As the body becomes more and more used to the substance so increasing amounts of it need to be taken to achieve the same effect.

A psychological and physical dependency together form the basis of an addiction. It is this vicious circle of dependency and addiction that needs to be broken if the drug habit is ever going to be beaten. The fight against dependency will go on throughout the addict's life. At no time will he or she be able to claim that they are 'cured'.

 Find out

Find out about the work amongst drug addicts carried out by one Christian charity. Write up notes about its work in your folder.

Beating the addiction

Serious drug addicts find that their addiction has led to a whole range of problems apart from the addiction itself. They are probably homeless, jobless and friendless. Their drug addiction can never be beaten unless real help is given with these other problems at the same time. This is why the drug addict needs social as well as medical support and help. In the past many Christian charities have set out to provide this all-round help for those in real need.

About 80 hospitals in the United Kingdom offer medical help to those who are addicted to drugs. A few of them offer in-patient support but the vast majority run out-patient Drug Dependency Clinics. A person may be referred to one of these clinics by their own doctor to attend voluntarily or be compelled to attend one by a court order. The treatment on offer is either:

1] A gradual withdrawal through cutting down on drug intake by prescribing a substitute which is less dangerous.

2] A total and sudden withdrawal of the drug. This causes severe withdrawal symptoms and intense distress.

Whatever method of withdrawal is followed the addict requires much support and care from others. This is often supplied within a community of similar sufferers and this community is often run along Christian lines. Christians are deeply concerned whenever a person abuses their own body [see box 1] as they see this as a denial of God's demand that one should look after the body since it is 'a temple of the Holy Spirit.

BOX 1

1 CORINTHIANS 3.16-17; 6.20

Do you not know that you are God's temple and that God's Spirit dwells within you? If anyone destroys God's temple God will destroy him. For God's temple is holy and that temple you are... You are not your own; you were bought at a price. Therefore honour God with your body.

▶ **Work to do**

1 Comment on one passage of the Bible which might have something to say about the problem of drug abuse.

2 Read the passage in box 1.
a. What does Paul describe here by the phrase 'God's temple'?
b. What does Paul say will happen to anyone who is responsible for destroying God's temple?
c. What do you think these verses might have to say about drug addiction - and any form of addiction?

4 Do you think that Christianity might have something to offer drug addicts. If so what?

2:7 Smoking

KEY QUESTION

WHY DO PEOPLE SMOKE AND WHAT ARE THE MAIN DANGERS OF THE HABIT?

Tobacco is thought to have been brought into England for the first time in the 16th century by Sir Walter Raleigh. In 1997 29% of adult males and 28% of women smoked – a considerable drop on the figures in 1970. People aged between 20 and 34 are most likely to smoke with 40% of men and 33% of women regular smokers. Less than 20% of people over the age of 60 smoke. Almost 70% of those who do smoke say that they would like to give up the habit.

Of more concern is the number of children and young people who smoke. The likelihood of a boy or a girl being a regular smoker increases with age and, at all ages between 11 and 15, girls are more likely to smoke than boys. By the age of 15 35% of girls and 25% of boys are regular smokers. However, girls smoke less cigarettes in total than boys. Boys of 15 who are regular smokers smoke an average of 56 cigarettes a week compared with 47 for girls. Each cigarette smoked takes, on average, six minutes off a person's life.

[A] Why do most people start to smoke?

Why do people smoke?

There are many reasons why a person might start, and continue, to smoke:

1] Nicotine, one of the ingredients in every cigarette, is addictive. Many people try to give the smoking habit up and fail.

2] To relax. Many people associate a cigarette with a time in the day when they stop working, pour themselves a drink and relax. This association is very important.

3] For pleasure. People who are trying to give the habit up will tell you that the most difficult situation to handle is when they are out with their friends socialising in an atmosphere heavy with cigarette smoke.

4] To conform. This is particularly important amongst young people and is a major reason why people start smoking. When friends light up it is not easy to be a nonconformist.

5] From habit. Smoking is habit-forming before it becomes addictive. Habits are difficult enough to break leave alone addictions.

The health risks

The risks to health of constant smoking have been well publicised. Each year about 50,000 people die in this country alone from illnesses related to smoking – about eight times the number of people killed each year on the roads. The main health risks from smoking are in these areas:

1] Bronchitis and Emphysema A lack of breath when taking the simplest forms of exercise is a common result of smoking.

BOX 1

KING JAMES 1. 1604

Tobacco taking is a custome loathsome to the eye, hatefull to the nose, harmfull to the braine, and dangerous to the lungs.

It has been said that 'smokers are very selfish people who only think of themselves.' What do you think the speaker meant and do you agree with them?

1 Describe what happens when a person smokes a cigarette.

2 Why do you think that smoking has been described as a social problem as well as a personal addiction?

3 What is the relationship between smoking and a person's health?

4 Many Christians smoke. What arguments do you think a Christian non-smoker might put forward to persuade them to give up smoking?

[B] Why do you think that so many young people smoke when the health risks are so well-known?

2] Coronary heart disease Each year 40,000 people under the age of 65 die prematurely from heart disease and at least 75% of these deaths are smoking related.

3] Cancer Over 300 people a week die from lung cancer and 9 out of every 10 of these people are heavy smokers. The nicotine and tar in cigarettes are carcinogenic i.e. they create the conditions which can lead to cancer.

Cigarettes are so dangerous because each cigarette contains over 40 poisonous substances, including nicotine, tar and carbon monoxide. The result of inhaling this poisonous cocktail is that the heart-rate is speeded up, the body is deprived of necessary oxygen and the tubes of the lungs are blocked by tar.

It is thought that it costs the country about £250 million each year to deal with the direct consequences of smoking.

Smoking and the Christian

Some religious groups have always been strongly opposed to smoking. The Salvation Army, for instance, does not allow its full-time officers to smoke. Most Churches, though, leave it up to the discretion of individuals to make up their own minds. Perhaps they have in mind the words of Jesus: "… not what goes into a mouth defiles a man, but what comes out of the mouth, this defiles a man." [Matthew 15.11]. Having said this many Christians would feel that there are strong reasons for dissuading fellow believers from committing what has been described as 'slow-motion suicide'. In part this is so that they can fulfil their responsibilities to others – whether a husband or wife, children etc. Young people find it easy to discount the risks of smoking because they are uncertain and distant. Christians, though, would not accept that this allows a person to escape from their responsibilities to God or to other people.

BOX 2

1 CORINTHIANS 6.19,20

Do you not know that your body is a temple of the Holy Spirit, who is in you, whom you have received from God? You are not your own; you were bought at a price. Therefore honour God with your body.

47

2:8 Alcohol [1]

KEY QUESTION

WHAT IS ALCOHOL AND WHY DO MOST PEOPLE DRINK IT?

Drinking alcohol – and suffering the after-effects – was certainly a popular pastime amongst the ancient Greeks and Romans. You can read what the ancient Epic of Gilgamesh, which dates from Babylonia in about 2525 BCE, had to say about alcohol in box 1. There are many references to alcohol, and its dangers, in the Bible [see unit 2.9].

What is alcohol?

Alcohol is made by the action of yeast on sugar. Yeasts are microscopic fungi which are carried in the wind. Wine is made when the yeast on the surface of grapes breaks down the sugar in the juice in a process called 'fermentation'. Wine is between 10% and 12% alcohol. Beer is made from cereal grain through a process of brewing and fermentation and is between 4% and 7% alcohol. Spirits are drinks which contain a large amount of alcohol brought about by 'distillation'. Spirits are between 40 % and 55% proof alcohol.

The body and alcohol

Alcohol is a drug because, once imbibed, it alters the chemical composition of the body. Unlike other drugs, though, alcohol is a legal drug. Rather than banning it we try to contain it by having strict licensing laws. When taken alcohol is absorbed quickly from the stomach and enters directly into the blood-stream. It is then carried around the body, so reaching the brain and all other body tissues. Alcohol is slowly removed from the blood stream by the liver where it is broken down into simpler chemicals. Water is removed from the body in the urine whilst carbon dioxide leaves through the lungs during breathing. The breakdown of the alcohol produces energy because alcohol is high in calories. Alcohol does not, however, provide the body with any useful nutrients – witness the beer-guts of many middle-aged men.

In the body alcohol:

1] Slows down the working of the brain so affecting the way a person speaks, thinks and acts. This is why drinking alcohol and driving a car are a lethal combination.

2] Affects the liver. The liver, an essential and irreplaceable organ, can cope with small amounts of alcohol. Large quantities, over a period of time, damage it permanently. Cirrhosis of the liver is the most common cause of death amongst heavy drinkers.

3] Damages the heart. A small amount of alcohol increases the blood pressure and pulse rate. In increasing quantities it increases the risk of a heart attack by building up fatty deposits around the heart.

BOX1

THE EPIC OF GILGAMESH

Sweet drink will put far away their cares. As they drank liquor their bodies became satiated. Much they babbled and their mood was exalted.

[A] What is the alcoholic content of beer, wine and spirits?

Talk it over

Do you think that most people have a sensible attitude to drinking alcohol or do far too many exceed the sensible limits?

4] Depresses the nervous system. Alcohol is, contrary to popular opinion, a depressant not a stimulant. It might initially stimulate and relax but it soon depresses the emotions.

5] Affects the stomach. Whilst a small amount of alcohol may help digestion large quantities can damage the stomach.

Alcohol, young people and women

In most Western countries around 90% of adults drink alcohol regularly. Young people, between the ages of 16 and 24, drink more heavily than adults. They are more likely to become drunk than adults because they are affected by fewer drinks. Young people have less body fluids than adults and this intensifies the effect of alcohol on them. In recent years heavy drinking amongst women has increased. 14% of women now regularly exceed sensible limits compared with 9% in 1984. The problem is made worse by the fact that women are more easily affected by alcohol than men. They weigh less than men and have less body fluids to dilute the alcohol. Their livers remove alcohol from the body less quickly.

BOX 2

ANCIENT JAPANESE PROVERB

First the man takes the drink, then the drink takes a drink, then the drink takes the man."

Work to do

1 What effect does drinking alcohol have on the body ?

2 Why are most Christians unhappy to see the effects of excessive drinking - especially on young people?

3 a. Why do you think that young people drink more heavily than adults?
b. Why does alcohol have a greater effect on young people than adults?
c. Why does alcohol have a greater effect on women than men?

[B] The vast proportion of alcohol is drunk in social gatherings. Why do you think that the two things so often go together in our society?

2:9 Alcohol [2]

Although some people drink large amounts of alcohol regularly this does not necessarily mean that they are dependent on it or addicted to it. Many people are able to go without alcohol if they cannot afford it or have been advised to stop drinking. Others, though, do not have their drinking under strict control. Worldwide about 1 in 15 people [7%] have a drink problem. This totals about 400 million people. There is nothing new in this. It was recognised in the Old Testament that many people drank too much [box 1]. One of the best descriptions of the effects of over-drinking comes from the same passage [box 2].

[A] Some people blame the easy availability of alcohol today as a major reason for the increase in alcoholism. Do you agree with them?

The dangers of heavy drinking

Medical authorities have decided that sensible drinking must be below 21 units of alcohol for men and 14 units a week for women. It is thought that 35% of men in the 16-24 age-group and 22% of women have a weekly intake above the sensible limits. Alcohol is directly responsible for bringing 30,000 lives in Great Britain to a premature end each year.

There is a strong link between alcohol and:

1] Domestic violence In more than half of all cases of wife-battering and child abuse alcohol is a major factor. This leads, in many cases, to the break-up of the marriage. Drinking by young people living at home also contributes to many families breaking up.

2] Road accidents and crime The law recognises that only small amounts of alcohol are needed to impair a driver's judgement. In all road accidents where the driver is killed 25% of them were over the alcohol limit. In 1997 this was over 900 people - almost three a day. It is estimated that 25% of all youngsters in detention centres have a serious drink problem.

3] Work problems In Great Britain about 15 million working days are lost each year through drink-related absence.

Alcohol dependency and teetotalism

1] Alcohol dependency About two million people in Great Britain are dependent on alcohol. This means that they resort quickly to drinking alcohol, especially when they are under stress. They return to normal drinking afterwards but resort to heavy drinking again if the situation changes. Of this number of people some 850,000 are medically classified as alcoholics. These are people who drink excessively and regularly and who suffer 'with-drawal symptoms' if they do not drink. Such people need the specialist help that such organisations as

BOX 1

PROVERBS 23.20

Do not keep company with drunkards or those who are greedy for the fleshpots. The drunkard and the glutton will end in poverty; in a state of stupor they are reduced to rags.

Talk it over

Given the unhappiness that drinking alcohol can bring do you think it surprising that more people do not follow the teetotal line?

Alcoholics Anonymous provide with its strong support structure. Such support is essential if a person is to find an answer to their drink problem.

2] Teetotalism Few Christians would be happy to see unchecked drinking leading to a breakdown in human relationships. Most Christians argue for sensible drinking [temperance] and this is the position supported by most Christian Churches. Some, though, believe that the dangers of drinking alcohol are so great, and the cost in human unhappiness of excessive drinking so high, that the only sensible attitude is teetotalism[total abstinence]. The Salvation Army, which has a wide experience of working with addicts of all kinds, makes teetotalism the rule for all of its officers. Other denominations, such as the Baptist Church, insist that only unfermented grape juice, rather than alcoholic wine, is used in the service of Holy Communion.

There are three main reasons why some people are teetotallers:

a. Whilst alcohol is not wrong in itself its misuse is. All Christians have a responsibility for their use, or misuse, of God's good gifts.

b. Christians have a responsibility to use their money wisely for God - and it would be very difficult to justify spending it on alcohol.

c. Christians have a responsibility to others around them. Drinking alcohol brings enormous social and personal problems which no Christian could feel happy about. The only sensible, and Christian, thing to do is to follow the line of teetotalism.

[B] What are the signs that someone is drinking too much?

BOX 2

PROVERBS 23. 29-32

Whose is the misery? Whose the remorse? Whose are the quarrels and the anxiety? Who gets the bruises without knowing why? Whose eyes are bloodshot? Those who linger late over their wine, those always sampling some new spiced liquor. Do not gulp down the wine, the strong red wine, when the droplets form on the side of the cup. It may flow smoothly but in the end it will bite like a snake and poison like a cobra.

Work to do

1 What dangers of drinking were the writers of the Old Testament particularly aware of?

2 Describe the attitude of two Christian Churches to alcohol.

3 Comment on two passages from the Bible which are relevant to alcoholism.

4 Do you agree with some Christians who argue that alcohol is best avoided all together because of its dangers?

5 a. What is teetotalism?
b. Why might many Christians argue in favour of teetotalism?

2:10 | Gambling

KEY QUESTION

WHY DO SO MANY PEOPLE FIND GAMBLING ADDICTIVE?

It is estimated that 4 out of every 10 adults in the U.K. gambles regularly. Men are twice as likely to be regular gamblers as women. The National Lottery began in November 1994 and over £100 million is spent weekly by 6 in every 10 households in Britain. Each household spends an average of £4 each week on the lottery. Of each £1 lottery ticket bought:

- 28p goes to good causes.
- 50p goes to winners.
- 22p goes to the organisers.

What is gambling?

Gambling is the investment of a sum of money in a game of chance in the hope of winning more at the expense of those who lose their investment. In Britain gambling can take one of four forms:

1] Gaming The playing for money in a game of chance whether poker, backgammon, roulette or any other. Gaming can take place privately but the stakes are likely to be higher if the game is played in a casino.

2] Betting This is the staking of money on an event, such as a horse or greyhound race, where the outcome is uncertain.

3] Lottery The distribution of prizes by lot or chance.

4] Football Pools These are a combination of 2 and 3.

Gambling is an ancient habit. Knucklebones, the original dice, have been found as far back as the 16th century BCE. Ivory, porcelain and stone dice - many of them 'loaded' - were found in the ruins of Pompeii. Soldiers gambled at the foot of the cross of Jesus for his clothes.

Why do people gamble?

Among the attractions of gambling are:

1] Excitement. It provides the instant excitement that many people, especially young people, crave. This explains the popularity of fruit machines, to which many young people become addicted, and the initial popularity of scratch cards attached to the National Lottery [A]. Interestingly, though, the popularity of scratch cards took a sharp nose-dive within a few months of them being introduced to the market.

2] Instant wealth. For the vast majority of people wealth is unobtainable through work and so 'games of chance' are the only means of bringing it within reach. The odds against it actually happening are, of course, depressingly long but 'someone has to win'. In fact, the odds against all six numbers coming up in the National Lottery are about 14 million to one but that doesn't stop people dreaming. Vast wealth brings a kind of power and most people would like to be powerful.

3] Relief from boredom. For most

[A] Why do you think that the popularity of scratch cards soon passed?

BOX 1

1 TIMOTHY 6.9,10

People who want to get rich fall into temptation and a trap and into many foolish and harmful desires that plunge men into ruin and destruction. For the love of money is the root of all kinds of evil. Some people, eager for money, have wandered from the faith and pierced themselves with many griefs.

[B] Do you feel that we still have an uneasy relationship with the presence of betting in our society?

people life is a constant struggle of making ends meet and gambling brings a frisson of excitement into mundane, humdrum everyday lives.

Unfortunately gambling, like alcohol, is difficult to control. A small stake in a raffle for a good cause is unlikely to hurt anyone. Nor is the occasional flutter on a horse race or a weekly investment in a pools accumulator. Controlled gambling allows a person to bring some colour and excitement into their life. Gambling, though, which gets out of

 Work to do

1 What is gambling and what are the different forms that it can take?

2 Which do you think are the most vulnerable groups in society to gambling and why might gambling be dangerous to them?

3 Can you explain why so many people gamble?

4 What do you think is the great attraction of gambling to so many people?

5 What is the Christian attitude to gambling?

control can destroy marriages, work, families and lives. Gamblers Anonymous, the organisation which helps people addicted to gambling, estimates that over 100,000 people in this country alone have such an addiction.

The Christian attitude

The attitude of the different Christian Churches towards gambling is similar to that which they have towards alcohol. The traditional Christian opposition to all forms of organised gambling has declined in recent years. There are still those who believe that the command of Jesus to his followers to love their neighbour must rule out any attempt to profit at their expense – and that is what gambling does. This remains the case even if the 'neighbour' is a willing participant. Others, though, would look at the situation in terms of the harm done. Obviously it is wrong to take money from someone if, as a result, they and their family go without food or other essentials. If, however, the money lost is 'leisure' money then little harm is done. At the same time, Christians are very much aware that gambling can be a dangerous activity and lead to some form of addiction. In particular, they are unhappy about the love of money which is the basic motivation behind most gambling. They believe this to be a very unhealthy, and unspiritual, approach to life [see box 1]

> **BOX 2**
>
> **LUKE 23. 33,34**
>
> *When they came to the place called the Skull, there they crucified him, along with the criminals - one on his right, and the other on his left. Jesus said, "Father, forgive them, for they do not know what they are doing." And they divided up his clothes by casting lots.*

Psalm 50.12; Mark 10.17-21; Matthew 6.24; Luke 12.15;Luke 18.25.

2:11 | Money and Wealth

Wealth is shared out very unequally in to-day's world. About 1 billion people, 1 in 6 of the total population, live in absolute poverty. This means that they do not have enough money to provide even the most basic necessities of life for themselves and their family. People in some African and Asian countries, for example, have incomes which are barely 2% of those enjoyed by people in Western countries. This is a situation that must concern each Christian deeply.

Materialism

We seem to live in a society in which material goods benefits are all that matter. 'Materialism' is the approach to life which attaches such a high level of importance to money and wealth.

Christians believe that materialism is contrary to the teachings of Jesus. They do not suggest that money does not matter – simply that other aspects of life are more important. Without money people suffer from poverty, hunger and homelessness. Most Christian charities attempt a modest redistribution of wealth by encouraging the rich to give some of their money to help the poor.

[A] What is materialism?

Money and wealth in the Bible

The Bible has more to say about wealth, and its dangers, than almost any other subject. It certainly figured prominently in the teaching of Jesus. Here are just four examples:

1] The Sermon on the Mount [Matthew 5-7]. Jesus encouraged the rich to share their wealth with the poor secretly. [Matthew 6. 1-4]. If they did this then God would reward them openly for their generosity. People were not to spend their whole lives amassing wealth since it is 'treasure in heaven' rather than wealth on earth that matters in the end. [Matthew 6.19-24].

2] The Rich Young Ruler [Mark 10.17-27]. When a wealthy young man approached Jesus asking to become a disciple he was told that only his money stood between him and the kingdom of God. The advice that Jesus gave him may seem harsh [box 3] but it shows how important it is to put God before everything else. Jesus went on to reinforce this message to his disciples [box 2].

3] The Parable of the Rich Fool [Luke 12. 16-21.] This story is about a man who spends his whole life amassing great wealth. Jesus wonders who will inherit this wealth when God decides that the man's life should end. A man's life is not to be measured in terms of his earthly wealth but in the depth of his relationship with God.

4] The Widow's Mite [Mark 12.41-44]. Jesus sat down opposite the place where people made their offerings to the Temple in Jerusalem. After watching many people put large sums into the treasury Jesus saw a poor widow putting in two small copper coins. Jesus told his disciples that she had put in 'more' than all the others since they had

---

BOX 1

MATTHEW 6.24

No-one can serve two masters. Either he will hate the one and love the other, or he will be devoted to the one and despise the other. You cannot serve God and Money.

1 How unevenly is wealth distributed in the modern world?

2 a. How prominently did wealth and money figure in the teaching of Jesus?
b. What did Jesus have to say in the Sermon on the Mount about wealth - and its proper use?
c. What did Jesus try to teach about money, and its dangers, in his encounter with the rich young ruler?
d. What did Jesus say about money, and its true value, after he saw a poor widow put money in the Temple treasury.

3 How do you think the teaching of Jesus about money was influenced by his own poverty?

given to God out of their wealth but she had made her offering from her poverty.

Paul also had much to say about wealth - and its dangers. Writing to Timothy, a young church leader, Paul commented: "The love of money is the root of all evil." [1.Timothy 6.10].It is noticeable that Paul did not trace all evil to money but to the 'love of money'. That would seem to be perfectly in keeping with the teaching of Jesus. He suggested that it is the love of money which prevents a person from giving away his wealth to help those who are poor and in need. Its hold is so strong that it even prevented someone from entering the kingdom of God.

BOX 2

MARK 10.24

Children, how hard it is to enter the kingdom of God. It is easier for a camel to go through the eye of a needle than for a rich man to enter the kingdom of God.

Talk it over

Do we now live in a society where material wealth and possessions are all that matter?

Usury

The Citizen's Advice Bureau has reported that it now advises more people about debt, and the way to get out of it, than any other problem. Most of these people have borrowed money, at a high rate of interest, and are unable to meet the repayments. In the Old Testament this was called 'usury' and was forbidden because of its unfairness to the poor. It simply made the rich richer - as it does to-day.Amongst the many laws which God gave to the Jews was one relating to usury: "If you lend money to one of my people among you who is needy, do not be like a money-lender; charge him no interest." [Exodus 22.25].

BOX 3

MARK 10. 21

Go, sell everything you have and give to the poor, and you will have treasure in heaven. Then come, follow me.

[B] How do many Christians attempt a modest redistribution of wealth in the modern world?

Proverbs 6.6-11; Matthew 20. 1-16; John 13. 14-15; 2.Thessalonians 6. 6-12

2:12 Why Work?

Work is any kind of endeavour, paid or unpaid, which involves mental or physical effort. The Victorians believed that hard work was important in itself and carried a high moral value. Everyone had a God-given duty to use the talents they had been given to the very best of their ability. The idea that hard work is important in itself is called 'the Protestant work ethic' – expressed in the old saying that 'The Devil finds work for idle hands to do'. Usually the virtue of hard work was linked to that of 'thrift' i.e. the need to save as much as possible and not to waste any money. The perfect citizen was the person who worked all the hours that God sent and had a thrifty approach to life.

Why work - the Christian attitude?

1] Work is essential. It is important that people work to satisfy their own need for clothing, food and shelter – and the needs of those dependent on them. Paul took a hard line on this [box 2] saying that if a person is not prepared to work then he should not eat. They cannot expect others to support them. Paul himself reminded his listeners that he came to them as a servant preaching the Christian Gospel and yet he also plied his trade as a tent-maker so that he was not a burden to anyone.

2] Work is fulfiling. Work is the main way that human beings have of finding a sense of achievement and self-fulfilment. God himself was the great creator who received much personal satisfaction whilst creating the world - time and time again we are told that God looked at his work

---

BOX 1

PROVERBS 6.6-11

Go to the ant, you sluggard; consider its ways and be wise! It has no commander, no overseer or ruler, yet it stores its provisions in the summer and gathers its food at harvest. How long will you lie there, you sluggard? When will you get up from your sleep? A little sleep, a little slumber, a little folding of the hands to rest - and poverty will come on like a bandit and scarcity like an armed man.

BOX 2

2 THESSALONIANS 3.10-13

We gave you this rule: If a man will not work, he shall not eat. We hear that some among you are idle. They are not busy; they are busybodies. Such people we command and urge in the Lord Jesus Christ to settle down and earn the bread they eat.

---

and saw that it was 'good'. He was happy with the work of his hands. Men and women have been made in the image of God and so are, at heart, creative beings. They receive an enormous blessing by using their talents to the glory of God and their own personal satisfaction.

3] Work is a social activity. Work provides an opportunity for most people to enjoy working with others. It can also be a way of serving others. Each person has a part to play in the work of building up the community, maintaining the environment and making sure that everything is ready to hand on to the next generation. The natural environment needs the graft of hard work. The community of which we are a part benefits from the work that we do on its behalf. We gain satisfaction from seeing a job well done. Everyone benefits from having a satisfied and fulfiled work-force.

Unemployment

From what has been said it follows that people who are out of work and unemployed are denied the opportunity of finding satisfaction through their work. Unemployment brings many pressures and may lead to the destruction of relationships. Families break-up and marriages end in divorce through unemployment. People begin to question their own self-worth [see unit 2.13].

[A] How important is the principle of serving others in most occupations?

Work to do

1 What is the Protestant Work Ethic?

2 What line did Paul take on the relationship between work and having the basic necessities of life?

3 What personal satisfaction is it intended that human beings should receive from their work?

4 What is a vocation?

5 Is leisure important?

Vocation

A vocation is a job that a person does because he or she believes that they have a 'calling', usually from God, to that occupation. In secular life the term is usually applied to one of the 'caring professions' such as nursing, teaching or social work. In a religious sense it can be applied to those who take vows and enter a Religious Order i.e. monks or nuns. More about this in unit 2.14.

Leisure

People need time to rest their bodies and minds. This is a time for re-creation when people are free to spend their time as they wish. It is this which marks leisure out from work. Hard work may well be involved in a leisure activity but it is hard work that is freely chosen and unpaid. More about leisure in unit 2.15.

BOX 3

COLOSSIANS 3.23

Whatever you do, work at it with all your heart, as though you were working for the Lord and not for men.

2:13 | Unemployment

KEY QUESTION

WHAT ARE THE MAIN CAUSES AND RESULTS OF UNEMPLOYMENT?

The International Labour Organisation [ILO] defines an unemployed person as someone who is without a job and is available to start work within two weeks. They have either looked for work in the previous four weeks or are waiting to start a job they have already obtained.

The unemployed

In Spring 1998 1,800,000 people were unemployed in the United Kingdom. This was a gradual decline since the highest recent figure of 2,900,000 in 1993:

1] The most common reason for becoming unemployed was given as redundancy i.e. being made unemployed by their employer. Other common reasons were a temporary job coming to an end, resignation, dismissal and health reasons.

2] Young people are much more likely than older people to be in search of work. Unemployment amongst 18 to 24 year olds runs at double the overall rate. Those between 16 and 17 are three times more likely to find themselves out of work than those between 60 and 64. The most likely reasons for young people being unemployed are lack of qualifications, skills and experience. Those without any advanced educational qualifications are four times more likely to find themselves out of work than those with qualifications.

3] Unemployment amongst white people is significantly lower than that amongst all ethnic groups. Amongst young black people, for instance, the unemployment rate in 1997/8 was 39%. For those aged 45 and over it was Pakistani/Bangledeshi people who suffered the highest unemployment rate at 26%. The unemployment rate for adult men of Asian and Afro-Caribbean origin is twice that of whites.

The causes of unemployment

To some extent the rate of unemployment is regional. The highest rates of unemployment in the United Kingdom are found in Scotland, Wales and Northern Ireland. There are three main reasons for high levels of unemployment in the last decade:

1] An increase in the number of people seeking employment, especially the number of women wishing to return to work.

2] The explosion of mechanisation and automation in the work-place. Large numbers of people in banking and insurance, for instance, have lost work in recent years as computerisation has been applied to these 'service industries'. This is a trend which is certain to continue.

3] The decline in manufacturing industries. Often since the early 1980s such industries as shipping and mining have lost out to foreign competition.

The effects of unemployment

The effects of unemployment are both personal and social:

1] **The personal impact** A distinction has to be drawn between short-term and long-term unemployment and its effects. Most people can survive unemployment for a month or two without suffering many ill-effects but when it goes on for months or years the effect can be catastrophic - a loss of self-respect, declining personal morale, tension with family members especially a spouse, a breakdown in family life, a lack of money, divorce, drug-taking, alcohol abuse and suicide.

2] **The social impact** Few people are left unaffected by long-term unemployment. In areas of high unemployment there can be many social problems - criminal behaviour, vandalism, burglaries, violence, rioting, racial abuse and attacks etc. Crime rates increase as the gap between rich and poor grows.

BOX 1

ECCLESIASTES 3.11-13

He has made everything beautiful in its time. He has also set eternity in the hearts of men; yet they cannot fathom what God has done from beginning to end. I know that there is nothing better for men than to be happy and do good while they live. That everyone may eat and drink, and find satisfaction in all his toil - this is the gift of God.

[A] Which kind of people are most likely to find themselves unemployed and looking for work?

Work to do

1 What is unemployment?

2 What are the most common reasons for people losing their employment or being unable to find a job?

3 Why do you think that unemployment is significantly higher amongst ethnic groups than amongst white people?

Christian involvement

The Church is one of the few organisations which is represented in every inner-city area where unemployment is likely to be high. As a consequence the Church often finds itself playing a central social as well as spiritual role. It may find itself providing food, clothing and housing for those without adequate means of support: setting

Talk it over

Do you agree with those people who maintain that unemployment is one of the most personally destructive things that can happen to a person? Why?

up schemes to help people use their enforced leisure time constructively such as running computer courses; running counselling centres to help the unemployed cope with their situation and organising 'job clubs' which seek opportunities for those without work to find employment.

Christians believe that creative and enjoyable work is part of God's plan for everyone. They believe that to deny such work to men and women is to frustrate this divine plan [box 1]. Clearly there is no easy answer to unemployment but Christians argue strongly that every effort should be made to find suitable employment for the unemployed – and that adequate support should be provided for those who genuinely cannot find work.

BOX 2

2 THESSALONIANS 3.10

For even when we were with you, we gave you this rule: "If a man will not work, he shall not eat."

2:14 Vocation

The word 'vocation', from the Latin word 'vocare' meaning 'a calling', is important in illustrating the Christian approach to work. The word itself is used in two different ways:

1] Many people feel that they have been called by God to do a certain job. At an early stage in his ministry Jesus called individuals to follow him and become his disciples. These people were in a variety of occupations such as fishing and tax-collecting but they responded to the demands of Jesus. In a similar way many Christians today feel that God has called them to do the work they do. The word 'vocation' is used traditionally to refer to the 'caring professions' such as being a doctor, a nurse or a teacher. These professions are singled out because they require a single-minded devotion to work without the financial rewards measuring up to the commitment and dedication required. The caring professions make heavy physical and emotional demands on those doing them and the work is very 'people-centred'.

Unfortunately, there is every reason to think that society takes such professionals very much for granted. Long hours, for example, are expected of workers in the medical profession. Junior hospital doctors, to take one example, work a minimum of 68 hours a week and are on call for 48 consecutive hours. This compares with an average working week in Britain of 35 hours. Doctors and nurses, though, can hardly go on strike! In any civilised society there must be a special provision to look after those workers who play a unique, and particularly important, role.

2] Some occupations are called 'vocations' and this refers, in particular, to those who believe they have been called by God to a religious vocation. To take just three examples:

a. Men and women in the priesthood are said to have a 'calling' which is tested in several ways before they are ordained into the Church. In the Roman Catholic Church only a male calling to the priesthood is recognised but almost all Protestant Churches now recognise the callings of both men and women.

b. Missionaries have responded to the 'calling' which God has given them to serve him full-time. A missionary is sometimes sent to work amongst people in their own country e.g. the London City Mission which works amongst the needy in the capital city. Sometimes a person feels called to serve God overseas. Nowadays such people are highly skilled taking their medical, teaching or agricultural skills to places where they are desperately needed. Often people from overseas feel called by God to serve him in this country.

c. A religious vocation to be a monk or a nun.

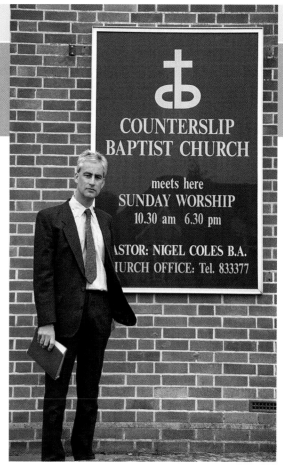

[A] Do you think that some people still feel 'called' to their work?

BOX 1

MARK 10.43-45

Jesus said, You know that among the Gentiles the recognised rulers lord it over their subjects, and the great make their authority felt. It shall not be so among you, whoever wants to be great must be your servant, and whoever wants to be first must be the slave of all. For the Son of Man did not come to be served but to serve, and to give his life as a ransom for many.

Do you think that society takes for granted the work of those people who have a vocational call to their work. How do you think that it can make sure that such people are treated fairly?

1 a. What is a vocation?
b. Describe ONE kind of work that you would describe as a vocation.
c. What makes this kind of work different from other jobs?

2 a. Why do you think that men and women called to be priests are said to have a vocation?
b. How do missionaries show that they have a vocation?
c. What does the word vocation mean when it is applied to men and women who join a Religious Order?

BOX 2

COLOSSIANS 3.23

Whatever you are doing, put your whole heart into it, as if you were doing it for the Lord and not for men.

Although most monks and nuns serve the Roman Catholic Church there are also many who serve God in the Anglican Church. Usually such vocations are considered to be for life although, increasingly, men and women are leaving their Religious Orders, often to marry. To do this they must break the vow of chastity which, along with those of poverty and obedience, they took when they entered the Order.

In this talk of vocation there is a danger in forgetting the genuine Christian attitude towards all work. God has given all people different skills but this does not mean that one occupation is more important than any other in the will of God. Every Christian, whether a doctor or a mechanic, a secretary or an accountant, has a vocation to carry out their work to the glory of God [box 2]. The vocation to which every Christian is called is to further the kingdom of God on earth. You can read what Jesus himself said about those who are going to do this effectively, whatever their occupation [box 1]. They are to follow in the footsteps of Jesus by walking humbly before every one and giving a life of service to all.

[B] Which three vows does a monk, or a nun, take to show their single-minded dedication to God and the service of others?

2:15 | Leisure

KEY QUESTION

WHY IS LEISURE TIME SO IMPORTANT IN THE MODERN AGE?

Most people today in Great Britain have far more leisure time than their ancestors did a century ago. The average working week is now 38 hours compared with 80 hours in 1900. This statistic, though, can be misleading. Some people, including mothers with little children and those caring for elderly parents or a disabled child, have little leisure time. The latest statistics, though, suggest that most people have 5 hours free on each working day and 8 hours at weekends.

Leisure in the Bible

The Jews were told by God that the Sabbath Day, the day of rest, was instituted because God himself had rested after spending six days creating the world. There were to be two characteristics of this special day [box 1]:

1] It was to be a 'holy' day. The word 'holy' means 'set apart' and, for Jews, this day was to be set apart, and so different, from the other six working days.

2] It was to be a day of total rest. Jewish rabbis classified over thirty activities as work and these were forbidden. Strict penalties were imposed on those found breaking the Sabbath laws

The early Christians were mainly Jewish and they continued to observe the Sabbath Day. In the 4th century, however, all the links between the Jewish and Christian faiths were broken and

Sunday [the day of the sun] was adopted by Christians as their holy day. This day, the first day of the week, was chosen because it was the day on which Christians believed that Jesus had risen from the dead. By worshipping God together on this day they were showing how important this event was for them. Although Christians do not keep Sunday as a day of complete rest most of them try to spend some time in church worshipping God on this day.

Leisure through the ages

The amount of time that people have to spend on their leisure activities, and the things that they choose to do, depend to a large extent on their age. Sociologists speak of five distinct 'ages' of leisure:

1] Childhood/teenage. Apart from elderly, retired

BOX 1

EXODUS 20.8,11

Remember the Sabbath Day, to keep it holy. Six days you shall labour and do all your work; but the seventh day is a sabbath to the Lord your God; in it you shall not do any work... for in six days the Lord made the heavens and the earth, the sea and all that is in them and on the seventh day he rested. Therefore the Lord blessed the Sabbath Day and declared it holy.

[A] How do you think people might prepare themselves for retirement - and all the free time they suddenly have?

[B] Why do you think it is so important for young children to learn to play together?

people those in this phase have more leisure time than anyone else. The main activities centre around spending time with friends, sporting activities, watching videos and T.V. and simply 'playing'[B].

2] Early married life. Spare time is usually spent setting up a home, having children, DIY, cooking, gardening. This is the age-group which has least spare time and this remains the case until children have a real measure of independence.

3] Early middle age. This is usually the time when people have most money. They, or their partner, has reached their maximum earning capacity. With the children being older and so more independent they are free to eat out more, join clubs associated with their hobbies or leisure pursuits, take more holidays etc.

4] Middle age. Children begin to leave home. People have time to devote to outside interests – church etc.

5] Old age. Leisure activities become less physical although walking is very popular. Knitting and gardening are two home-based activities. Playing with grandchildren is important.

Leisure is important at all stages in life. The 'workaholic' is someone who is likely to have many problems - not least health ones. The Biblical emphasis on the need to give the mind and body time to recover from the exertions of work develops into the need, as the person grows older, to have activities which occupy the mind and body. Boredom can be very destructive, whatever a person's age.

Too much leisure time, though, can also be a problem. The unemployed man or woman finds, after a while, that 'enforced leisure' is destructive. Many people, forced to retire at a certain age, would like to continue working - at least part-time. The abrupt change from full-time work to full-time leisure is very difficult for many to make. In an ideal society the transition from one to the other would be gradual so that people can make plans for their retirement and how they are going to spend it constructively and happily. [A]

 Work to do

1 List three activities: a. Which might be considered a good use of leisure.
b. Which might be considered a bad use of leisure time by Christians.

2 How do leisure interests and pursuits change as people grow older.

3 Describe one way in which a Christian might show that Sunday is a special day to them.

2:16 Homelessness

The United Nations Declaration on Human Rights states clearly that everyone has the right to enjoy a decent standard of living and the house in which they live is a very important part of this [box 1]. The Church of England Report 'Faith in the City' emphasised the need for housing to be of an adequate standard to give people real control over their lives [box 2].

Facts and figures

1] The number of dwellings in the United Kingdom rose by 50% between 1961 and 1997 – and now totals 24,800,000. About 25% of these houses, though, were built before the First World War and in some inner city areas this figure can be as high as 60%. Thousands of these houses are in urgent need of repair or demolition.

2] About 17 million dwellings are owner-occupied and about 8 million rented.

3] According to 'Social Trends 29', an official government publication, 96% of people feel reasonably secure in their homes although crime, hooliganism and vandalism were mentioned as three main causes of insecurity.

4] About 3 million people are thought to be without suitable,and adequate, housing in the UK. but worldwide [A] there are at least 150 million people without adequate accommodation in which to live.

Homelessness

The number of families in 'priority need' of housing in the United Kingdom for which local authorities accepted responsibility in 1997 was 108,000. This was the lowest figure for ten years having dropped steadily from 1992 [146,000]. Of

BOX 1

UNITED NATIONS. DECLARATION ON HUMAN RIGHTS

Everyone has the right to a standard of living adequate for the health and well-being of himself and of his family, including food, clothing and housing.

 Talk it over

What do you think a family needs for their housing to be described as 'adequate' ?

the number in urgent need of housing in 1997 57% had dependent children and 1 in 10 had a pregnant woman in the house. 25% of these households were homeless because parents, other relatives or friends were no longer able, or were unwilling, to house them. A further 25% gave the breakdown of a relationship as the main reason why they were homeless. The majority of people, mainly women, in this last group stated that the violence of their partner was the reason why the relationship broke up.

Obviously these reasons are amongst explanations for many people, usually young, ending up sleeping rough on the streets. There are thought to be around 160,000 young people in this situation, the vast majority sleeping on the streets of major cities. In London alone there are thought to be 50,000 rough sleepers. Amongst the problems which force them into this situation are:

[A] What do you think it does to people themselves to live in housing like this?

Work to do

1 The United Nations Declaration on Human Rights states that everyone has the right to have adequate housing. Do you think this is a right for every human being?

2 Look at quotation 2.
a. How do you think that substandard housing might affect a person's security, privacy and ability to grow as people?
b. In what way might poor housing conditions affect a person's ability to make choices for themselves. Why would that be a bad thing?

1] Physical illness, preventing a person from working.
2] Mental illness, which makes it very difficult to cope with any pressure.
3] Money problems, which makes escape seem to be the only answer.

Once on the street people become easy prey to alcohol and drug-related problems. These seem to offer a temporary release from all other difficulties. Soon, of course, they become the source of a

Find out

Here are four organisations which help people, in some way, cope with homelessness - the Salvation Army, the Simon Community, the Cyrenians and Shelter. Find out about the work of ONE of them amongst the homeless and write up the notes in your folder.

whole new raft of problems. In 1999 the government committed itself to providing hostel accommodation for everyone who wanted it in the foreseeable future.

Shelter and the Big Issue

Shelter was formed as a major charity dealing with homelessness in 1966 after a television play 'Cathy Come Home' had stirred the conscience of the nation. Since then the charity has worked with homeless people to reach lasting solutions to the problem. It has sought to publicise the needs of homeless people and to encourage government action to make life easier for them. It has also sought to give practical help on a local level by providing debt counselling, access to medical facilities, furniture for unfurnished accommodation and other kinds of assistance. The 'Big Issue', a magazine sold by homeless people on the streets, was launched in 1991. The idea is that the homeless buy their own copies of the magazine and then sell them, at a profit, on the streets. By providing homeless people with some income they have the opportunity of buying basic necessities and finding accommodation.

BOX2

CHURCH OF ENGLAND REPORT 'FAITH IN THE CITY'. 1985

A home is more than having a roof over one's head. Decent housing certainly means a place that is warm and dry and in reasonable repair. It also means security, privacy, sufficient space, a space where people can grow and make choices... Vandalism, graffiti, fear of violence, lack of play space, all affect how people regard their surroundings. How property is managed, as well as the physical condition is important as it affects how people make decisions. To believe that you have no control over one of the most basic areas of your life is to be devalued.

2:17 The Disabled

If you could make ONE change in society which would improve the lot of the disabled what would it be?

KEY QUESTION

WHO ARE THE DISABLED AND WHAT PROBLEMS DO THEY HAVE?

According to government statistics, there are 6.2 million adults [14% of all adults] and 360,000 children [3% of all children] who suffer from one or more disability. Of these people 34% are living in poverty. The term 'disability' covers three groups of people:

1] THE MENTALLY HANDICAPPED One form of mental handicap is that of Down's Syndrome, caused by the addition at birth of an extra chromosome to each cell. Although Down's Syndrome is not hereditary the chance of having a Down's Syndrome child increases with the age of the mother. There are 500,000 people in the UK who suffer from Down's Syndrome and other forms of mental handicap. Societies such as MENCAP [Royal Society for Mentally Handicapped Children and Adults] are able to put parents of mentally handicapped children in touch with other parents. Amongst the problems that parents face are:

- how their child is going to cope when they themselves are no longer able to look after them.
- other children in a family who may resent the additional attention given to the handicapped brother or sister.
- resentment that such a thing should have happened to them and a fear that they will not be able to cope with the many pressures.

2] THE MENTALLY ILL Mental illness is very different to mental handicap. The range of mental illnesses is huge. It can include a whole list of phobias - claustrophobia, agoraphobia etc. Autism and schizophrenia are illnesses which cut a person off from everyone else around them. Many old people suffer from Altzeimer's or Senile Dementia. Millions of people pass through depression at times. It is thought that one in six women and one in nine men suffer mental illness and need to consult medical help at some time in their lives for this problem. For many, though, it is a recurrent illness from which there is no final escape.

3] THE PHYSICALLY HANDICAPPED The vast majority of physically handicapped people do not need any kind of assistance but many do. These include the loss of or injury to limbs; blindness and deafness. About 6 in every 10 disabled people live in the world's developing countries. Many of them receive no help from the country in which they live - only from relatives and friends. Most have no chance of finding employment and they end up begging on the streets - a familiar sight in many developing countries. In this country disabled people may be unable to work or be limited to certain kinds of employment.

The International Year of the Disabled

In 1971 the United Nations set out the rights of all mentally handicapped people and, two years later, the rights of those who are physically handicapped. In 1981 the International Year of the Disabled was held under the motto 'Full participation and equality'. This was very helpful because it set out just what all handicapped people need if they are going to be able to participate fully in life on an equal basis with those who are able-bodied. There were five demands:

1] To do whatever is necessary to make it possible for the mentally and physically handicapped to participate fully in all aspects of life.

2] To support all national and international efforts to train disabled people so that they can lead as full a life as possible. All disabled people have the right to enjoy full employment opportunities.

3] To encourage shops and places of entertainment

BOX 1

THE LOCAL CHURCH AND MENTALLY HANDICAPPED PEOPLE. CHURCH OF ENGLAND REPORT. 1984

Mentally handicapped people have so much to give; they share our common humanity and, like us all, are children of God.

 Find out

Find out some information about the work of either the Cheshire or the Ryder Foundations. Write up some notes in your folders.

1 a. What do you think are the basic needs of disabled people?

b. Do you think that in to-day's society enough attention is paid to meeting those basic needs.

c. What do you think are the three most important things that society needs to do to help disabled people live as normal a life as possible?

2 Describe how service to disabled people might be an important expression of Christian love.

3 Do you think that it is important that disabled children should be encouraged to attend an ordinary school alongside able-bodied children. Consider both points of view on this issue, always looking at the question from the point of view of disabled children.

4 a. Do you think that children and adults with a disability suffer from prejudice and discrimination in our society.

b. If they do, what do you think is the cause of this prejudice and discrimination?

c. How would you set about doing something about the prejudice and discrimination?

to make access for disabled people a matter of high priority.

4] To educate able-bodied people about the needs and rights of the disabled.

5] To prevent disability as much as possible and to help in the rehabilitation of those who are disabled.

Help

There are many societies and charities dedicated to helping the disabled. Two of them, the Cheshire and Ryder homes, were founded by a husband and wife team. The Cheshire Homes, dedicated to helping those who are chronically ill, now works in over 50 different countries.

[A] Write down THREE things which make the life of blind people difficult in today's world.

2:18 The Elderly

Do you look on the prospect of growing old with unremitted gloom or do you think there are elements to compensate for the problems. If so, what do you think they are?

KEY QUESTION

WHAT PARTICULAR PROBLEMS DO OLD PEOPLE FACE IN OUR SOCIETY AND WHAT IS THE CHRISTIAN ATTITUDE TOWARDS THEM?

The largest group of people needing help and support in our society are the elderly. The number of people over retirement age in the United Kingdom is around 11 million, 18% of the total population. Between 1961 and 1971 the people in the population over 75 years of age grew from 4% to 7%. Of the people of retirement age:

- 52% live with their husband or wife.
- 36% live alone.
- 7% live with their children.

[A] From where do most of this group of elderly people receive their income?

Women form over 65% of elderly people. At the moment they draw their old age pension at 60 and men at 65. From 2020 onwards, though, all people in Great Britain will receive their old age pension at 65. Each man can now expect to live until 71 and each woman to 75. Throughout the world the United Nations estimates that, by 2025, one in seven people will be aged 65 or over – compared with one in twelve in 1951.

The problems of old age

There are four main problems associated with growing old:

1] Failing health Over 50% of all doctor's prescriptions are written out for the over 65s and this age-group makes, on average, 7 times more visits to their doctor than a person of 35. Diseases like arthritis, rheumatism and bronchitis are much more likely to affect the elderly. Life threatening illnesses like strokes, heart disease and cancer become, of course, much more likely as one grows older.

2] Poverty Once a person reaches retirement age they are almost certain to experience a considerable drop in income. 70% of pensioners depend on the State pension as their sole means of income. The State pension is only 15% of average male earnings. The older people are the poorer they are likely to be – with single and widowed women coming off worst.

3] Loneliness Well over 2 million elderly people live alone and the vast majority of these are

1 Write TWO sentences about each of the following in relation to older people:

a. The problem of poverty.

b. The problem of health.

c. The problem of loneliness.

d. The problem of death.

2 How would you sum up the attitude that Christians are encouraged to have towards older people?

3 We live in a world in which people are living longer and longer. List THREE future problems that this will cause.

[B] Why do you think it is important for elderly people to remain active for as long as possible?

women – most men are older than their wives when they marry and die, on average, four years earlier. Bereavement, being housebound or disabled brings a sense of isolation to many people living on their own.

4] Death Many old people no longer feel wanted. Although the fear of dying probably decreases with age nevertheless old people do find it difficult to cope with the increasing proximity of death as they see their friends and contemporaries dying.

The Bible and the elderly

The Bible might have little to say about the problems of old age such as we know them in modern society but it does lay down certain principles which govern the treatment of all older people – especially within the context of the responsibilities which children carry for their parents. This extends from the fifth Commandment [*'Honour your father and mother' Exodus 20. 12*] through to the advice given by Paul to the young Timothy [box 1]. It was natural that such advice

should be given to children since everyone at the time lived in an extended family network – in which everyone, young and old, had something valuable to contribute to family life. Many of the problems that the elderly face today would not have arisen in the extended family.

The Ten Commandments make it clear that children carried responsibilities for their parents for as long as they lived. In the 'Golden Rule' expressed by Jesus [*Matthew 7.12*] he made it clear that everyone should treat everyone else in the way that they themselves would like to be treated by them. Jesus criticised those religious laws which made it possible for a person to evade their responsibilities towards their parents by giving extra money to the Temple. Older people should have nothing to fear in any society based ultimately on the principle of love. Sadly, that is not always the case.

BOX 1

1 TIMOTHY 5.1-4, 8

Do not rebuke an older man harshly... Give proper recognition to those widows who are really in need. But if a widow has children or grandchildren, these should learn first of all to put their religion into practice by caring for their own family and so repaying their parents and grandparents, for this is pleasing to God... If anyone does not provide for his relatives, and especially for his immediate family, he has denied the faith and is worse than an unbeliever.

BOX 2

ROBERT BROWNING. RABBI BEN EZRA

Grow old along with me!
The best is yet to be,
The last of life, for which the first was made;
Our times are in His hand
Who saith 'A whole I planned,
Youth shows but half; trust God;
see all, nor be afraid!

2:19 | Sexism

KEY QUESTION

WHAT ARE THE REASONS FOR SEXISM IN SOCIETY AND IN THE CHURCH?

'Sexism' takes place every time a person, usually a woman, is discriminated against because of their sex. The Sex Discrimination Act of 1975 makes it unlawful to discriminate against people on sexual grounds in areas relating to recruitment, promotion or training. Job advertisements must not discriminate in their language but they can make it clear that they are looking for people of a particular sex. If, though, a person of either sex applies then they must be treated equally and fairly. Two exceptions were noted by the Act:

1] Women are not allowed to work underground.

2] Women may be debarred from the priesthood in the Church since some Churches believe that a male priesthood is a 'Genuine Occupational Qualification' [GOQ].

Reasons for sexual prejudice'

The working life of most women is affected by their function as mother as well as worker. Most of the sexual prejudice she is likely to suffer stems from this. Most women take a break from their career at some time to have children and bring them up. They can, if they wish, qualify for paid maternity leave which allows them to stay at home for 4 ½ months but many mothers do not return to work when this is finished. If this break is extended then a person might grow out of touch with the demands of their job and may need retraining. Employers often fear a high level of absenteeism from a mother who is trying to juggle the conflicting demands of work and motherhood. Sexual stereotyping still persists in some areas of the job market as certain careers are seen as being unsuitable for women – engineering, car mechanic etc.

Women priests

Most Free Churches, such as the Methodist and Baptist Churches, have had women ministers for a long time. The Church of England ordained its first women priests in 1994 but, as yet [2000], there are no female bishops. The Roman Catholic Church and the Orthodox Church have almost 60% of

Christian believers between them worldwide and they are totally opposed to the idea of women priests. The arguments in the debate can be set out clearly between those who hold a conservative view [against] and those who hold a liberal view [for] women priests. One wishes to keep things as they have always been whilst the other wants to see the Church make necessary changes in the modern world.

1] AGAINST WOMEN PRIESTS

a. Jesus chose twelve men to be his disciples and the Church is built firmly on their teaching. The Church cannot change the pattern that Jesus himself firmly established.

b. No single Church should act on such an important matter without the agreement of all the others. The opposition of the Roman Catholic and Orthodox Churches is firmly established. Pope John Paul 11 has said that the ordination of women in the Anglican Church sets Church unity back a long way.

c. When he is celebrating Holy Communion, the most important task of a priest, he is representing Christ and so must be male.

BOX 2

1 CORINTHIANS 14. 34-35

Women should remain silent in the churches. They are not allowed to speak, but must be in submission, as the Law says. If they want to enquire about anything, they should ask their own husbands at home; for it is disgraceful for a woman to speak in a church.

BOX 2

ST AUGUSTINE, 6th CENTURY

Any woman who acts in such a way that she cannot give birth to as many children as she is capable of makes herself guilty of that many murders.

1 Write about the attitude of Jesus towards women using the passages at the head of this unit to help you.

2 What is sexism?

3 What are the main arguments used by both sides in the debate about the ordination of women?

4 'Christianity treats women as second-class citizens'. Do you agree with this assessment?

2] FOR WOMEN PRIESTS

Other Christians believe that women priests the refusal of some Churches to ordain women is a prime example of sexism. They may be within the law but the Church should not be seen to treat the majority of its members as second-class citizens. The arguments in favour of the ordination of women are:

a. The Church as a whole should show that it is genuinely 'inclusive' giving an equal role, and equal opportunities, to both male and female.

b. The priest represents the whole people of God and so it is irrelevant whether the priest is male or female.

c. The Bible was written at a time when the role of women in society was very different to what it is today. The Church must either change with the times or die.

Paul, who wrote many of the books in the New Testament, is often put forward as a prime example of sexism. He certainly held some sexist ideas that people, including many Christians, would feel very uncomfortable with today [box 1]. So, too, have other Christian leaders in the past [box 2]. It is difficult to find any justification to-day for preventing women serving the Church alongside men, if that is what they believe God has called them to do.

[A] Do you think that many non-churchgoers find it strange that some Churches will not ordain women?

2:20 | Racial Prejudice & Discriminati

KEY QUESTION

WHAT ARE PREJUDICE AND DISCRIMINATION AND WHY ARE THEY SUCH DANGEROUS ATTITUDES FOR PEOPLE TO HAVE?

When we talk about racism, racial prejudice and racial discrimination there are four words which need to be defined, and understood, carefully. They are:

1] RACISM Racism is the belief that one race of people is superior to another. The supposed superiority may be a physical, intellectual or spiritual one. If a person holds this belief strongly then it will exert an enormous influence over the way that they treat other people.

2] PREJUDICE Everyone holds opinions and these can come from parents, school, church, friends or the mass media. Prejudice is an attitude of mind on any topic which encourages us to 'prejudge' those who differ from us in some way. Some of these opinions stem from a person's racial origins. Prejudice is in the mind but it also pre-determines how we act. If, for example, someone carries out a vicious attack on someone because they are the 'wrong colour' it will only be because they are prejudiced.

3] DISCRIMINATION Prejudice takes place in the mind but discrimination translates that prejudice into real-life. Racial discrimination takes place when a person is unfairly treated by others because of their racial origins. Britain, as many other countries, have outlawed the most blatant forms of racial discrimination in areas such as education, housing and employment but such discrimination is always difficult to demonstrate and prove.

BOX 1

SECOND VATICAN COUNCIL

The Church reproves, as foreign to the mind of Christ, any discrimination against people... on the basis of their race, colour, condition in life or religion.

4] SCAPEGOATING AND STEREOTYPING
Everyone is aware of the problems of poor housing and unemployment. The real explanations for these problems is too difficult for many people to understand. A simple answer is to blame everything on 'outsiders', such as racial minorities, who 'taking the jobs and houses' [see below]. The fact that this is basically untrue is ignored. These 'outsiders' become scapegoats.

Scapegoating and stereotyping are closely linked. Stereotyping takes place when a person links together all people from a race or group simply because he has observed certain kinds of

1 What is prejudice and how might it lead to discrimination?

2 Explain the difference between prejudice and discrimination.

3 a. What is racism?
b. Why do you think that discrimination can be such a dangerous attitude in our society?

4 a. What is scapegoating and stereotyping?
b. Give an example of stereotyping which is racially motivated.
c. Why do you think that stereotyping is such a dangerous attitude if it is allowed to go unchallenged ?

[A] Do you think that children are aware of racial differences?

behaviour in one or two representatives of that group. The stereotypes are then used as an excuse for attacking members of that group or discriminating against them.

Causes of prejudice

There are several reasons why racial prejudice is such a feature of modern life:
1] The influence of parents. Most racial prejudices are inherited early, at a time when the influence of parents is at its greatest. It is almost impossible to share a home with people without absorbing many of their basic attitudes to life.

2] Fear. In the 1960s and 1970s, when racial intolerance became so widespread, this country went through spells of high unemployment. At the same time many more black immigrants were allowed into Britain to live than is the case today. People feared that immigrants were living in the houses and doing the jobs that should have been theirs.

3] Ignorance. Although there are now about three million black and coloured people living in the UK they have tended to live in communities largely composed of their own people. The amount of integration between black and white has only been comparatively limited. This has left white people largely ignorant of the way that other people live. Human beings are often most afraid of what they don't know about or understand.

Prejudice and discrimination have a great influence both on those who are discriminated against and those who do the discriminating. It often creates feelings of anger and revenge in those who are at the sharp end of discrimination. This leads to the strong temptation to retaliate and take the law into their own hands. In some people who experience discrimination it leads to an inferiority complex. They come to believe the propaganda which is being pushed out against them. Eventually this leads to a feeling of alienation from society and from those around. People who suffer discrimination feel that they no longer belong to the society in which they live.

BOX 2

MARTIN LUTHER KING

An individual has not started living until he can rise above the narrow confines of individualistic concerns to the broader concerns of all humanity.

2:21 | Race in Britain

KEY QUESTION

WHAT DOES IT MEAN WHEN BRITAIN IS DESCRIBED AS A MULTIRACIAL SOCIETY?

Britain is a multi-racial and a multi-religious society. This enriches the life of the nation and of the individuals who live in it as long as two fundamental conditions are met:

1] All races in the country experience true equality in law.
2] All means of discriminating against minorities in such basic areas of life as education and employment opportunities are removed – in practice as well as in law.

If these two conditions are not met then racism exists. 'Institutional racism' takes place when the law protects in any way people who are racist. Frequent criticisms in recent years have been levelled against more than one police force in the United Kingdom that it is institutionally racist.

Immigration

From the mid 1950s immigrants began to enter Britain in large numbers in search of work and to escape persecution in their home countries. The government of Britain was very pleased to welcome them because there was a marked shortage of labour in certain industries after the Second World War. The British Nationality Act of 1948 had given United Kingdom citizenship to anyone born in a British colony. The influx of immigrants was halted by the Commonwealth Immigrants Act [1968] which allowed entry to British passport holders only if they were born, adopted, registered or naturalised British citizens or had a parent in one of these categories. The law was mainly passed to keep out East African Asians who were being persecuted in Kenya and Uganda – and who wanted a home in Britain.

Today there are about 2,500,000 black people living in Britain. They form about 4%, 1 in 25, of the total population. Most of them were born in this country. To protect them two Race Relations

BOX 1

DR GEORGE CAREY, ARCHBISHOP OF CANTERBURY

Racism has no part in the Christian Gospel. It contradicts our Lord's command to love our neighbours as ourselves. It offends the fundamental Christian belief that every person is made in the image of God and is equally precious. It solves no problems and creates nothing but hatred and fear.

▶ Work to do

1 Describe THREE ways in which it might be argued that being a multiracial society enhances the lives of people living in Britain.

2 Write ONE sentence about each of the following:
a. The British Nationality Act [1948]
b. The Commonwealth Immigrants Act. [1968] c. The Race Relations Act [1968] d. The Race Relations Act [1976]

3 Describe how black citizens of the UK might suffer in each of the following areas: a. Employment.
b. Education.
c. Housing.

Acts have been passed:
1] Race relations Act [1968] Made it illegal to discriminate against anyone because of their country of origin in employment, trades unions, housing or education.
2] Race relations Act [1976] Set up the Commission for Racial Equality to help people who suffered from discrimination at the hands of other people.

Discrimination

Racial discrimination takes place in four areas of life:
1] Employment. When black immigrants came to Britain in the 1950s and 1960s they were encouraged to come to fill largely unskilled or semi skilled jobs. These were jobs that white people were reluctant to take. The evidence today suggests that most of the people who came then are still in the same kind of employment.
2] Education. A report in the mid 1980s found that black children and young people were under-

performing at all levels of the educational system. The reason was partly the racist attitudes of their teachers who, often unconsciously, had much lower expectations of black children and were placing them in the lowest groups. There are comparatively few black teachers who are able to challenge these racist attitudes in schools.

3] Housing. Black people have suffered considerable discrimination in the housing market. Black people have traditionally lived mainly in the inner-city areas where most of the housing is rented. This has left them open to discrimination by white landlords when they are looking for tenants for their property. It has also allowed white housing officers working for local authorities to discriminate against black people in need.

4] The Social Services. Black people traditionally make far less use of the social benefits which are available because they are not aware of them or are afraid to ask for them. Many immigrants still speak imperfect English and this is a major obstacle to claiming benefits.

Prejudice still exists in this country although it is more difficult to find out if discrimination does. There is some evidence to think that the attitudes of people many be changing slowly. Surveys show that young people are less prejudiced than their parents. It remains true, though, that whilst laws can prevent obvious discrimination only a further change in the attitude of people can eradicate it.

BOX 1

WORLD COUNCIL OF CHURCHES. 1980

Every human being created in the image of God is a person for whom Christ died. Racism, which is the use of a person's racial origin to determine their value, is an assault on Christ's values, and a rejection of his sacrifice.

[A] What problems do you think a racially mixed family might encounter in this country?

2:22 | The Christian Perspective on F

Christians believe that God created all human beings equal – whether young or old, male or female, black or white [box 1]. God does not treat any human being as being more important than any other. Since prejudice encourages us to think of some people as being inferior to others it is a totally unchristian attitude. It cannot be justified in any circumstances.

Jesus and prejudice

During his lifetime Jesus said and did many things to show that he had no sympathy with prejudice in any area of life. To take three examples from the Gospels:

1] Healing the servant of a Roman officer *[Luke 7.1-10]*. The army officer was a Gentile [non-Jew] and so he sent some Jewish leaders to Jesus for help. He did not think that Jesus would welcome him as he wasn't a Jew. The leaders asked Jesus to heal the officer's servant as he was close to death. They told Jesus that the officer loved the Jewish nation and had built their synagogue for them.

Jesus, though, showed no interest in the man's background –
only in his faith. He told the people before healing the man: "I have not found such great faith even in Israel."

2] The parable of the Good Samaritan *[Luke 10.30-37]*. This was a story that Jesus told in answer to a question – 'Who is my neighbour'? In the story [A] a Samaritan saved the life of a Jew who had been beaten up and robbed by thieves on the road between Jerusalem and Jericho. Although Samaritans and Jews had much in common they had been sworn enemies for centuries. All relationships between them had broken down. By

[A] What can we learn from the parable of the Good Samaritan about the attitude of Jesus towards prejudice?

Talk it over

Do you think that it would make a tremendous difference to the way we treated other people if we believed that everyone is a child of God?

? Find out

Find out about one well-known Christian who has helped to fight racial prejudice. Write notes up in your folder.

setting a Samaritan at the heart of his story Jesus was indicating that a person's need should compel us to act – whatever the needy person's religion or nationality. True humanity and compassion pay no regard to secondary issues like a person's background.

3] In the time of Jesus there was prejudice and discrimination against women but Jesus, by his actions, showed that this had no place in the kingdom of God. A woman approached Jesus in Tyre [*Mark 7.24-30*] and asked him to heal her daughter. This was a very unusual thing to do in a society where women did not approach men in public and engage them in conversation. The woman's need for help, though, overcame any artificial barriers which had been placed in her way. When she showed that she was determined to overcome these barriers Jesus healed her daughter and told her that it was her faith that had brought about the girl's healing.

BOX 1

GALATIANS 3.26-28

You are all sons of God through faith in Christ Jesus, for all of you who were baptised into Christ have clothed yourselves with Christ. There is neither Jew nor Greek, slave nor free, male nor female, you are all one in Christ Jesus.

Peter's dream

Jesus seemed to imply at the beginning of his ministry that he had only been sent by God to help the Jews enter his kingdom. Soon, however, Gentiles were being welcomed as well but the early apostles, after the ascension of Jesus into heaven, found this difficult to accept. Peter, the early leader of the Christian Church, began to eat with non-Jews and he was heavily criticised for doing so. He answered by describing a vision in which a sheet had been let down from heaven [*Acts 10. 9-23*]. In the sheet there were all kinds of animals – "four-footed animals of the earth, wild beasts, reptiles and birds of the air" – which Jews were forbidden to eat by their laws. The voice that Peter heard from heaven told him to get up, kill and eat.

Peter replied that nothing 'impure' had ever crossed his lips but the voice of God reminded him that nothing created by God could ever be described as 'impure'. To treat any animal or group of people as 'impure' and less significant than others is completely unjustified. It is to close one's eyes to the truth. God created all forms of life and they are equally important to him.

The forms that prejudice took in the times of Jesus were largely sexual and religious. There is no evidence that he ever came across any prejudice based on social class or the colour of a person's skin. There is no reason to think, though, that his attitude to either of them would have been any different if he had. In the kingdom of God which Jesus came to build there is simply no room for any prejudice or discrimination.

▶ Work to do

1 a. What information from the Bible might a Christian use when trying to form their own ideas about racism?
b. Why do you think that these teachings are important for Christians in to-day's world?

2 Why would Christians think that prejudice was wrong?

3 "Jesus did not discriminate. Jesus was not prejudiced." Use Biblical material to support this statement.

4 a. Briefly outline Peter's vision about clean and unclean animals.
b. What did Peter learn from this vision about prejudice?

BOX 2

1 CORINTHIANS 12.12,13

The body is a unit, though it is made up of many parts; and though all its parts are many, they form one body. So it is with Christ. For we were all baptised by one Spirit, into one body - whether Jews or Greeks, slave or free...

2:23 | The Sanctity of Human Life

Christians believe that life is a gift from God and so is extremely precious and sacred. Men and women are made in the image of God and this makes them different from all other forms of life [box 1]. All human life is to be cherished and respected [box 2]. In the units that follow we will be trying to work out just what this means in practice in the modern world.

If you look at box 1 you will notice that:

1] Men and women were created 'in the image of God'. All other forms of life were created before human beings. After each species was created God was pleased with his work because he 'saw that it was good'. Nothing, though, was actually made in the divine image. Men and women are unique. They both bear a striking resemblance to God because they have a spiritual capacity denied to all other forms of life. As the Psalmist declares: "You made him [man] a little lower than heavenly beings and crowned him with glory and honour." [Psalm 8. 5].

2] Man is given dominion over all other forms of life [Psalm 8. 6-8]. This dominion stems from man's superior intellect and genuine freedom which is shared with no other species. Humankind can shape events whilst every other form of life can only respond to them. Power, however, always brings responsibility and humankind must exercise its God-given authority under the control of God.

Why respect human life?

Human beings must respect all forms of life. In particular, they must show the greatest possible respect for human life. This is because:

1] All men and women are made in God's image.

2] All human beings have been created to be equal by God. No one group is inferior to another. In any humane society equal respect must be given to the very young and the very old. This must be kept in mind when we are considering abortion [units 2.24 & 2.25] and euthanasia [2.28].

3] Jesus came to show God's love for all human beings. He died on the cross for everyone – without exception.

4] Every human being has an immortal 'spirit', the welfare of which is in the hands of God alone. No-one has the right to end the life of another human being prematurely – under any circumstances. Just as God decides the precise moment of a person's conception so he alone should decide the exact timing of their death.

Work to do

1 When Christians insist that human life is a gift from God, and sacred, what do you think they mean?

2 Read box 1 carefully.
a. When the Bible says that human beings are made in the image of God what do you think it means?
b. Man is said to be master of the created world. What kind of mastery do you think this should be?

3 Why do you think that the Church opposes all forms of discrimination?

BOX 1

GENESIS 1.26,27

God said, "Let us make man in our own image, in the likeness of ourselves, and let them be masters of the fish of the sea, the birds of the heaven, the cattle, all the wild beasts and all the reptiles that crawl upon the earth. God created man in the image of himself, in the image of God he created him, male and female he created them.

These Christian principles are very important when considering all questions of life and death. Before looking at them, however, it is important to remember that:

a. Whatever a person's age, state of health, educational achievements, intelligence-level or place in society they can, and do, make a unique contribution to its health and well-being. Without them the world would be a much poorer place. Their value to God is incalculable.

b. The Church must be totally opposed to any kind of discrimination which suggests that some people are more important than others. This means, for instance, that the mentally and physically handicapped must be cared for even though they may never make any economic contribution to society. The Church must always make sure that it speaks for those who are unable to protect themselves. The weak and the vulnerable should always be a major priority for the Church and those who live their lives by the teaching of Jesus. Of all Christian Churches the Roman Catholic Church maintains the strongest line on the sanctity of life. It condemns all unnatural forms of birth-control, abortion, suicide and euthanasia.

[A] Talking about the sanctity of human life what do you think is suggested by this piece of sculpture?

BOX 2

THE CATECHISM OF THE CATHOLIC CHURCH [2258]

Human life is sacred because from its beginning it involves the creative action of God and it remains forever in a special relationship with the Creator, who is its sole end. God alone is the Lord of life from its beginning to its end; no-one can under any circumstances claim for himself the right directly to destroy an innocent human being.

2:24 Abortion [1]

KEY QUESTION

WHAT IS 'ABORTION ON DEMAND' AND DOES IT EXIST IN THIS COUNTRY?

An abortion is an operation carried out on a pregnant woman to remove and destroy the foetus in her womb. Since 1967 it has been legal to do this in the UK as long as certain conditions are met. More abortions are performed in the UK per head of the population than anywhere else in Europe. Each year 13 abortions are carried out for every 1,000 women in the country.

Two Acts of Parliament

Before 1967 abortion was illegal in the UK. A large number of 'back-street' abortions, though, were carried out by unqualified people which put the lives of desperate women at risk. It is thought that when the Abortion Act was passed in 1967 the number of illegal abortions was more than 200,000 a year. Each year about sixty women died from these whilst thousands of others were severely injured or made infertile because of the way they were treated.

Under the Abortion Act abortion became legal if:
1] Two doctors agreed that an abortion was legal and the operation was carried out before 'the time of viability' i.e. the time when the baby could survive on its own outside the womb. At the time this was put at 28 weeks but the Human Fertilisation and Embryology Act of 1990 later lowered it to 24 weeks.
2] The continuation of the pregnancy would involve a greater risk to the mother or any member of the family than if the pregnancy was terminated.
3] A termination is necessary to avoid permanent

BOX 1

PSALM 139.13,14

You created my inmost being; you knit me together in my mother's womb. I praise you because I am fearfully and wonderfully made; your works are wonderful, I know that full well.

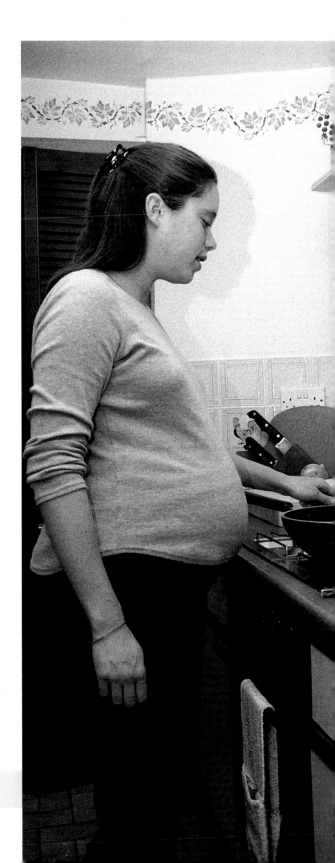

[A] This baby is wanted - and it will be loved and cherished. What factors might lead a woman to feel differently about the baby she is expecting?

1 a. What is an abortion?
b. Why was it considered necessary to introduce the 1967 Abortion Act?
c. Under what circumstances can a legal abortion now be carried out in the United Kingdom?

2 a. What is 'abortion on demand'?
b. Do you think that the current law seems to allow abortion on demand in this country?

3 Read quotations 1 and 2 carefully.
a. Put each of them into your own words to show that you understand what they are saying.
b. Do you think that they rule out abortion - or not?

injury, physical or psychological, to the mother. **4]** There is a real risk that the baby will be born handicapped or deformed.

Although an abortion can be carried out up to 24 weeks of pregnancy this rarely happens unless there is a very real medical emergency - an abortion rarely takes place after 22 weeks. The vast majority of abortions have taken place by the 12th week of pregnancy.

Abortion on demand?

Opponents of abortion argue that the Abortion Act made abortion so easy to obtain that it has virtually created 'abortion on demand'. It is true that few requests for an abortion now fall outside the law. The number of abortions performed in the United Kingdom reached 167,000 by 1973 but this fell back to 130,000 in 1976 only to rise steadily until 1990. Then, for the next five years, the figure began to decline. In October 1995 the Committee on the Safety of Medicines issued a warning that there were seven brands of contraceptive pill which carried a risk of thrombosis for women. As many women stopped taking the Pill on hearing this so more babies were conceived - and the abortion rate went up. By 1997 the number of abortions was greater than it had been before the scare.

The number of abortions carried out on women between the ages of 16 and 19 has seen the greatest increase since 1968. It was 2.5 abortions for every thousand women in this age-group in 1968 but is now 24.5 for every thousand - an increase of almost 1000%. For those girls under the age of 16 the abortion rate is much lower but it has still increased by 600% in the same time.

Drawing conclusions

Abortion divides people very strongly. As you will discover in 2.25 Christians are very divided on whether abortion is a modern necessity of life or not. Clearly before the 1967 Abortion Act became law the situation with so many women undergoing illegal, and highly dangerous, back-street abortions was totally unsatisfactory. Something needed to be done.

Supporters and opponents of abortion disagree strongly, though, over whether an abortion is simply too easy to obtain. Under the present law a woman can obtain one if she shows that her own health, physical or psychological, is at risk if the pregnancy continues. Since all birth 'affects' the psychological balance of the mother so this clause allows anyone to claim that an abortion would be legal. At the same time for a woman to continue with a pregnancy might well have an adverse effect on the rest of her life. The morality, or otherwise, of an abortion is extremely difficult to assess - and must ultimately be left to the mother. She must live with the consequences of her decision for the rest of her life.

BOX 2

UNITED NATIONS DECLARATION ON HUMAN RIGHTS

The child, by reason of his physical and mental immaturity, needs special safeguards and care, including appropriate legal protection, before as well as after birth.

2:25 | Abortion [2]

KEY QUESTION

WHAT ARE THE MAIN ARGUMENTS FOR AND AGAINST ABORTION?

Abortion is legal in the United Kingdom and in most Western countries. The issue remains, though, highly controversial. These differences of opinion in society are also reflected in the various Christian Churches.

Christian attitudes

The majority of Christians feel very unhappy about abortion. The Didache, the oldest known Christian document, was written about 70 CE and stated: "You shall not kill by abortion the fruit of the womb and you shall not murder the infant already born [infanticide]."

The Roman Catholic Church expresses the strongest objection of any Church to abortion. It teaches that abortion denies to a baby the most fundamental of all human rights - the right to exist. Life, the Church teaches, begins the moment a baby is conceived in the womb. The destruction of a foetus, however early in the pregnancy, amounts to murder since it destroys an organism that is already living. Any Catholic who is involved in an abortion, whether mother or medical personnel, is threatened with excommunication from the Church and its sacraments. The Catholic Church supports those organisations - such as LIFE and SPUC [Society for the Protection of the Unborn Child] which are involved in opposing abortion under all circumstances.

The Church of England, like other Protestant Churches, believes that abortion is an evil that should be avoided if at all possible. However, it can be justified if there is a risk to the physical or psychological health of the mother; if a deformed baby is likely to be born or if a woman has conceived a baby as a direct result of being raped.

Pro-Choice arguments

The main arguments in favour of giving a woman a free choice about abortion are:

1] Every woman has the right to do as she wishes with her own body. The foetus is part of that body up to the point when the baby is born. True life does not begin until a baby is recognisably human at the earliest.

2] Every baby has the right to be born into a family which can meet its basic needs for food, shelter and love. If a mother cannot offer these to her baby then an abortion is justified. Lone parents are amongst the poorest members of the community.

3] A handicapped baby requires total dedication and commitment from those who look after it for the whole of its life. Many parents cannot provide this and it is not fair to ask them to struggle to do so.

4] There are far too many unwanted babies in the world already. Why add to their number?

5] Other members of a family have their own rights as well and these must be respected. This extends to the husband and existing children as well as the mother.

6] A woman who becomes pregnant after a rape should not, under any circumstances, be forced to have the child of her attacker. There can be no justification for this.

Abortion is never an easy option. It requires a sensible and mature decision to be made. If the decision is made to go ahead with an abortion

---

BOX 1

MOTHER TERESA

I am sure that deep down in your heart you know that the unborn child is a human being loved by God like you and me. If a mother can kill her own child what is there to stop you and me from killing each other?

 Find out

There are organisations which promote abortion and those which oppose it strongly. Find out about the arguments used by ONE organisation from each side and the way that it goes about its work. Write up your notes in your folder.

1 What are the differences between the Roman Catholic and the Protestant approaches to abortion?

2 What are the main arguments which could be put forward to support making abortion legal?

3 What are the main arguments put forward by those people who are opposed to abortion?

BOX 2

THE SECOND VATICAN COUNCIL

God, the Lord of Life, has entrusted to men the noble mission of safeguarding life… Life must be protected with the utmost care from the moment of conception: abortion and infanticide are abominable crimes.

then a high emotional price will be paid. Every person must be allowed to do this without coming under any outside pressure.

Pro-Life arguments

The main arguments against abortion are:

1] Every child is a gift from God to be loved and cherished. It is unthinkable that anyone should destroy such a gift.

2] Abortion is murder – the killing of another human being. It is the killing of a human being who cannot defend itself in any way [see box 1]

3] Everyone, especially those who are vulnerable in society, need special protection and have the right to expect it. The rights of the unborn child are at least equal, if they do not exceed, those of the mother.

4] A foetus is a human being from the moment it is conceived. It has a perfect right to live. If the foetus is damaged in some way it still has the same right.

Aborting a baby often destroys a mother's peace of mind for a long time and lays heavy on their conscience. It would be far better for someone who is pregnant, and does not want to keep the baby, to offer it up for adoption. There is a shortage of such babies and a long line of couples who cannot have children of their own waiting to adopt.

[A] Do you think that anyone could have an abortion without being deeply affected by what they are doing.

2:26 | Assisted Conception

KEY QUESTION

HOW DO THE
CHRISTIAN
CHURCHES
RESPOND TO
DIFFERENT WAYS
OF ASSISTING
CONCEPTION?

The marriage service underlines the importance of having children as one of the main reasons for marriage [1.12]. 10% of couples, though, cannot have children because either the man or the woman is infertile. To overcome this problem in 1997 33,520 couples sought medical help and in over 6,000 of the cases the woman became pregnant. As this treatment is not available on the National Health each couple paid an average of £3,000 for this help. In some cases the treatment was repeated when it proved unsuccessful on the first occasion.

If a couple is infertile there are three possible options open to them and each one of these raises some moral or religious questions:

1] AIH [ARTIFICIAL INSEMINATION BY HUSBAND]

AIH applies when tests show that the man is healthy but that his partner is not releasing an egg for fertilisation or, more likely, that the sperm cannot reach the egg to fertilise it. In this case sperm can be taken from the man and implanted in the woman's uterus. The egg is fertilised by the sperm and the pregnancy continues normally.

Comment: Those opposed to any assistance being given to the reproductive cycle argue that this is unnatural – and so against the will of God. This opinion involves accepting that a couple's infertility is the will of God so it is wrong to try and alter the situation. Another argument is that infertility is nature's way of keeping the population down. Against this it seems natural for most couples to want a family and in AIH science is simply giving a helping hand to those couples who would otherwise be infertile. The fact that the sperm comes from the husband would seem to overcome most moral objections to AIH.

2] AID [ARTIFICIAL INSEMINATION BY DONOR]

AID takes place when the woman is fertile but her partner is not. He may not be providing enough healthy sperm to fertilise his partner's eggs and so conception cannot take place. It is one of the mysteries of life in Great Britain that the sperm count of most men is much lower than it was a decade or two ago and so infertility is higher. To overcome this problem an anonymous donor provides healthy sperm which are used to fertilise the woman's egg and the foetus grows normally in her womb. Clearly the baby born will share genetic characteristics with its mother but not with her husband or partner.

Comment: AID raises more serious ethical and religious questions than AIH. If the woman alone is physically related to the baby can they both claim to be its parents in the same way? This would not worry some couples. They would simply be delighted to have a baby. Some Christians, especially Catholics, though, would argue that AID is little more than a sophisticated form of adultery. The Roman Catholic Church opposes both AIH and AID [box 1] although the Church of England is happy to accept them – with safeguards. In particular, the Church of England opposes AID if

---

BOX 1

POPE JOHN PAUL 2

Techniques of artificial conception are morally unacceptable, since they separate procreation from the fully human context of the conjugal [sexual] act... the number of embryos produced is often greater than that needed for implantation in the woman's womb, and these so-called 'spare embryos' are then destroyed or used for research which, under the pretext of scientific or medical progress, in fact reduces human life to the level of simple 'biological material' to be freely disposed of.

1 'Humankind is interfering with nature by using I.V.F. techniques to help couples to have children and that is very dangerous.' Do you agree with this comment?

2 What is:
a. Artificial insemination by husband?
b. Artificial insemination by donor?
c. In vitro fertilisation?

3 Explain THREE moral or religious issues raised by scientific involvement in the conception of a baby.

4 Read box 1. Summarise, in your own words, the arguments used by Pope John Paul 11 for opposing all forms of 'assisted conception'.

What do you think about the arguments which say that infertility is nature's way of keeping the population down or is the will of God?

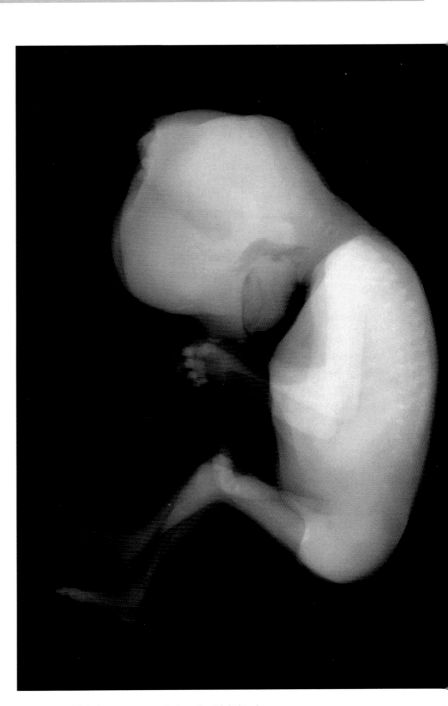

[A] Do you think that every couple has the 'right' to have a baby?

any payment of money is made to the donor and insists that central records are kept so that any children conceived in this way can find out the identity of their real father when they reach the age of eighteen if they wish.

3] IVF [IN VITRO FERTILISATION]

Both AIH and AID take place within the woman's body. In IVF, though, fertilisation takes place in the laboratory and the fertilised egg is then placed back in the woman's uterus. The first time this happened successfully was in 1978 and it is now a common procedure.

Comment: Those who support the use of IVF argue that as the woman's egg and the man's sperm are used in the procedure it does not matter where conception takes place - inside or outside the body. Often, though, IVF is used in conjunction with a donor's sperm because the partner's sperm are damaged, or unhealthy, in some way. The Human Fertilisation and Embryology Act, 1990, regulated matters so that no human embryo could be kept alive outside a woman's body for more than 14 days.

There are also other techniques used by science to assist the conception of babies. There is 'surrogacy' [womb-leasing] where a woman carries a baby for nine months and then gives birth for a couple who cannot have a baby. The couple take the baby over after birth. There is also 'embryo donation', where a fertilised egg, with both donors unknown, is placed back into the woman's uterus.

2:27 | Suicide

Suicide is a sad fact of modern life. Many people, in this country and elsewhere, take their own lives:

1] Until 1961 suicide was illegal in this country. Anyone who attempted to take their own lives, and failed, could be prosecuted and sent to prison after being nursed back to life. This was very cruel. It is still illegal for someone to help someone else take their own life [assisted suicide].

2] Suicide rates across the UK have fallen slightly in the last 15 years, except amongst men between the ages of 15 and 44. For both men and women the suicide rate in Scotland is considerably higher than that for the rest of the United Kingdom.

3] Suicide among men is about three times higher than amongst women. Men aged 15 to 44 are four times more likely to take their own lives than women of the same age. Suicide becomes less likely for men as they grow older but more likely for women. Women over the age of 45 are 40% more likely to commit suicide than those under 45.

Why do people take their own lives?

Suicide is the most extreme human act and people are usually driven to it for the most extreme reasons. Amongst the most common reasons for suicide are:

1] Money worries - personal, business etc.

2] Loneliness - often as the result of the death of a loved one.

3] The loss of work - redundancy.

4] Divorce - the break-up of a family, the threat of divorce, divorce proceedings, the loss of the family home, problems with access to children etc.

5] Old age - the loss of physical and mental faculties.

6] Depression - disease, terminal illness, alcohol and drug abuse.

7] Pressures at school - exam failure, bullying etc.

Suicide is often a 'cry for help'. This means that the person committing the act really hopes that they will be stopped, or discovered, before it is too late. Perhaps they have tried to tell someone about their problem and have not been taken seriously. Suicide, or the threat of it, is often a desperate attempt to make people listen.

[A] Does it surprise you that many people who take their own life are young?

Talk it over

The Samaritans is staffed by volunteers. What kind of person do you think would make the ideal Samaritan volunteer?

BOX I

JOB 12.10

In his hand is the life of every creature and the breath of all mankind.

1.CORINTHIANS 10.13

No temptation has seized you except what is common to man. And God is faithful; he will not leave you to be tempted beyond what you can bear. But when you are tempted, he will also provide a way out so that you stand up under it.

The Samaritans

The Samaritans is the main charity working amongst people considering suicide. It was formed in 1953 by an Anglican priest, Chad Varah, who discovered just how many people were committing suicide in his own East End of London parish. To begin with he publicised a telephone number in his church that anyone could ring, day and night, if they needed help. He soon found himself overwhelmed by the number of calls that he received. This was the beginning of the Samaritans - a name taken deliberately from the parable of the Good Samaritan told by Jesus *[Luke 10. 30-37]*. The Samaritans is not a Christian organisation although many of the workers may be Christian believers. They are not allowed to speak about their faith in case they embarrass those seeking help.

Today there are branches of the Samaritans in most cities in the UK - over 200 altogether. The telephones in these centres are staffed totally by volunteers who offer a listening ear to anyone thinking of taking their own lives. A strict anonymity is maintained between volunteer and client. Volunteers are known only by their Christian names and are expressly forbidden to enter into a close relationship with someone in need. Each year over 2.5 million phone-calls are made to the Samaritans in the UK.

BOX 2

A SAMARITAN VOLUNTEER

Volunteers have to resist their natural impulse to solve some desperate cases by giving material help and comfort... they have to accept that when a client swears to phone next day they will often break their word... they have to accept that weeks, and even months, may be spent on a case without a word of gratitude... they must remember that a person they have helped will often not even remember their name. The volunteer will find from bitter experience that he or she is often what they choose to be - faceless, nameless, just a voice or an ear on the end of a phone and nothing else.

Christians and suicide

In the past Christian Churches have taken a very strong line against suicide. Believing all life, and especially human life, to be a gift from God it has remained a serious sin for someone to take their own life. The Roman Catholic Church, in particular, has taught that suicide is a 'mortal sin' and serious enough to prevent the guilty person from entering heaven. They could not receive the blessing of a church funeral nor be buried in 'consecrated ground'. Today, though, the Churches take a more sympathetic line recognising the pressures under which many people have to live.

Work to do

1 Why do Christians think that suicide is wrong?

2 What are the main reasons for people deciding to take their own lives?

3 a. Who are the Samaritans?
b. What work do the Samaritans do?

4 Discuss these two points of view:
a. "Only God has the right to determine the exact time when a person dies."
b. "Every man and woman must have the right to take their own lives if life becomes intolerable."
Which of these two statements do you agree with? Explain why.

5 Read Luke 10.30-37. Why do you think an organisation working amongst those thinking of taking their lives was called the Samaritans?

2:28 | Euthanasia

Euthanasia is the right to seek ' a good, easy death' and is illegal in the United Kingdom. 'Voluntary euthanasia' is that in which the person concerned, or some one to whom that person has given authority, authorises the ending of their life. This will only be when a terminal illness becomes an impossible burden for them to carry.

For and against voluntary euthanasia

1] FOR VOLUNTARY EUTHANASIA

a. It is a basic human right that a person should be able to choose the moment at which they die. This decision could be made at a time when death was not imminent and could be withdrawn at any time. Friends and relatives could be consulted about the decision

b. Faced with a terminal illness, for which there is no cure, everyone should be able to have a quiet, dignified and relatively painless exit from the world. All too often death is a deeply distressing experience for everyone involved. Voluntary euthanasia spares relatives and friends from much anguish at the end of a loved one's life.

The Voluntary Euthanasia Society [now known as EXIT] has argued for voluntary euthanasia for a long time. It argues that doctors should be able to help incurable patients die if that is their express wish. To safeguard against abuse patients should have signed a form requesting this at least 30 days earlier. Such a change in the law would remove the threat of later legal action being taken against the doctor - a threat which often prevents them from acting in a humane way.

2] AGAINST VOLUNTARY EUTHANASIA

a. There are now ways in which pain can be controlled and people allowed to die with dignity - without voluntary euthanasia. This has coincided with the growth of the Hospice Movement [see unit 2.30].

b. Human beings do not have the right to decide the time of their own death since this decision belongs to God alone. This is an argument that appeals to Christians, especially Roman Catholics, who are strongly opposed to euthanasia [see box 1]. They believe that human beings have immortal souls which return to God when a person dies.

c. Legal euthanasia would place doctors in an impossible situation since it would ask them to do something that is against the 'Hippocratic Oath' - the oath which they take when they begin their medical careers and which commits them to save life.

1 Describe, and explain, the teaching that a Christian would bear in mind when considering euthanasia.

2 a. What is meant by euthanasia?
b. State TWO reasons why most Christians would be opposed to euthanasia.

3 a. What arguments are put forward to support voluntary euthanasia?
b. What arguments are put forward to oppose voluntary euthanasia?
c. Explain which of these arguments you find most persuasive - and why.

d. Legal euthanasia would be an intolerable burden on elderly people leading them to believe that they had nothing left to contribute to society.

Euthanasia and the Christian Church

As boxes 1 and 2 make clear the Christian Churches are opposed to the legalisation of euthanasia. Their role is to bring the light and love of Christ to everyone – young and old, fit and unwell. As Jesus himself showed in the New Testament the major work of his disciples is to extend God's love to those who need particular care and help. This is to help the handicapped, the sick and the elderly to live as normal a life as is humanely possible. Whatever its motives euthanasia is certain to lead to the curtailing of the lives of

[A] Do you think that people should have the right to decide for themselves when they want their lives to end?

many of these people. The Church cannot even contemplate this possibility because:

1] Euthanasia does not show a true respect for God – who is the creator and end of all human life. Human beings ignore this truth at their peril.

2] God created human beings as being a little lower than the angels and of infinite worth and dignity. To remove them from the earth by a simple injection is a grave sin.

3] Euthanasia is murder and that is against the Ten Commandments.

4] Everyone knows that doctors withhold treatment from a patient if that simply extends a meaningless existence. There is a wealth of difference, however, between this and actively killing a person. Painkillers should be used to relieve pain even if this means shortening the life of a patient but doctors can go no further than this. This is known as the 'law of double effect'. The whole of a patient's needs in his or her final hours must be met [box 2] by those responsible for their care.

BOX 2

METHODIST CONFERENCE 1974

The argument for euthanasia will be answered if better methods of caring for the dying are developed. Medical skill in terminal care must be improved, pre-death loneliness must be relieved, patient and family must be supported by the statutory services and by the community. The whole of the patient's needs, including the spiritual, must be met.

2:29 The Hospice Movement

In the Middle Ages hospices were small institutions that looked after the elderly, the sick and travellers. Most of these hospices had a Christian foundation since the spiritual care of the sick and dying has always been a major task undertaken by the Church. The physical care of the sick and dying has also been undertaken by Religious Orders of monks and nuns. This work has continued in recent years through such devoted workers as Mother Teresa and her Missionaries of Charity in India.

The modern Hospice Movement

The modern Hospice Movement began when a group of Irish nuns, the Sisters of Charity, established a home for the dying in Dublin towards the end of the 19th century. In 1900 five nuns from this Order travelled to London to continue their vocation of caring for the terminally ill in the East End of London. Within a few years they had established the St Joseph's Hospice. Almost sixty years later a young nurse, Cicely Saunders, went to work at St Joseph's. Her nursing career was cut short by a serious back injury but, in 1967, she established the St Christopher's Hospice in London. There are now about 100 in-patient hospices in England offering, at any one time, care for some 2,000 patients who are terminally ill. In the USA the first hospice was opened in 1974 and now about 2,000 hospices look after the needs of 300,000 patients.

The aims of the hospice movement

Whatever their religious background hospices have the same basic objective - to offer care and support for patients, friends and relatives, at the most difficult time in their lives. Within this overall objective the Hospice Movement has three aims:
1] To relieve pain - whether caused by the illness itself or by the fear and anxiety of approaching death. Hospices specialise in pain control. Doctors and nurses working in hospices have led the way in palliative care [the control of pain by drugs] in recent years. It is a basic principle of each hospice

BOX 1

THE CATECHISM OF THE CATHOLIC CHURCH

Those whose lives are diminished or weakened deserve special respect. Sick or handicapped persons should be helped to lead lives as normal as possible... Even if death is thought to be imminent, the ordinary care owed to a sick person cannot be legitimately interrupted... Palliative care is a special form of disinterested charity. As such it should be encouraged.
[2276.2279]

that all pain, no matter how acute it might be, can be brought under control by using drugs properly. The Catholic Catechism sees this as an essential element in the care of anyone who is approaching death [see box 1].
2] To enable patients, relatives and friends to face up to approaching death. Hospices, and those who run them, see this as one of the most important reasons for their existence. It is very important that people face up to their anxieties and fears about dying. In our society death remains the last genuine taboo subject. Few people are able to speak about it openly. Although most hospices have a Christian foundation no attempt is made to persuade patients to believe in God. Hospices are open to people of all religious faiths - and none.

Talk it over

Hospices do such an important work in looking after those who are dying that their work should be supported financially by the State." Do you agree?

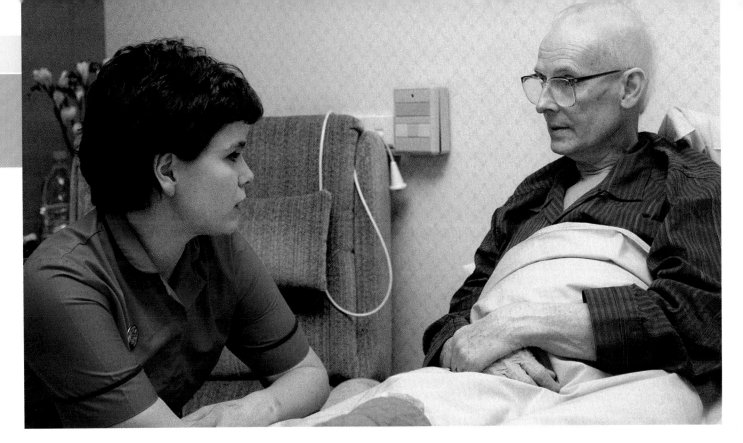

[A] What is the basic principle on which the Hospice Movement is based?

3] To care for the mental and emotional needs of relatives and friends. In modern hospitals, with the emphasis on the prolonging of life, these needs are often forgotten - or ignored. A hospice seeks to meet them - both before and after a patient has died. In this way it helps considerably with the grieving process.

How hospices help

The number of hospice beds available in the United Kingdom is much less than demand. As a result most of them can only offer short-term care. To begin with patients often enter a hospice for a week or two to give their carers some respite. Then, as their physical condition begins to decline, so they enter the hospice for a longer time. At the end of this time they can choose whether to spend their last few days in the hospice or at home. This is an important part of hospice philosophy. It leaves the patient a real measure of independence and choice whilst, at the some time, offering the care and support that those approaching death need. If they choose to die at home they can still make use of the facilities and support of the hospice. Macmillan Nurses, who are attached to many hospices, visit patients in their own homes. The emphasis is firmly on death with dignity wherever that death might take place.

BOX 2

DR CICELY SAUNDERS

Anything which says to the very ill that they are a burden to their family and that they would be better off dead is unacceptable. What sort of society could let its old folk die because 'they are in the way'?

 Work to do

1 Why do many Christians support the work of the Hospice Movement?

2 How do Christians offer help to those people who are terminally ill?

3 Do you think that people who are terminally ill should be told that they are dying? Give as many reasons as you can for your answer.

4 a. What is distinctive about the help and support provided in a modern hospice?
b. What does a hospice set out to achieve?

5 In box 1 the Catechism of the Catholic Church describes palliative care of the dying as 'a special form of disinterested charity'.
a. What is palliative care?
b. What do you think is meant by 'a special form of disinterested charity'?

2:30 | Suffering

1 Make as complete a list as possible of examples of:
a. Mental and emotional suffering.
b. Physical suffering.

2 Write an essay of about 600 words carrying the title 'The problem of suffering'.

3 a. Describe the Christian attitude towards suffering.
b. Explain whether or not you find this attitude convincing. Give as many reasons as you can for your answer.

4 Look at quotation 1 carefully. What point is this extract from Job making about suffering? Do you agree with it? Explain your answer.

KEY QUESTION

WHAT PROBLEMS DOES THE UNDENIABLE FACT OF WIDESPREAD SUFFERING CAUSE TO THOSE PEOPLE WHO ARE CHRISTIANS?

Sickness and suffering are amongst the most serious problems that any believer in God has to face. Sickness brings everyone face to face with their own mortality and powerlessness. As the Catholic Catechism points out: "Every illness can make us glimpse death."

Examples of suffering

Suffering is a universal experience since no-one escapes it in some shape or form. Take four examples:

1] Natural disasters – floods, earthquakes, volcanoes etc. These natural disasters kill thousands of people each year and the human race has no control over them. They usually hit the poorest and most vulnerable people.

2] Adults and children dying each year through hunger and malnutrition – simply because they have been born in the wrong place. Malnutrition is directly responsible for the deaths of 20 million people each year.

3] Children who are born with incurable illnesses or massive handicaps through no fault of their own or their parents.

4] Illnesses or accidents which rob families of parents or children.

There are many examples of suffering which could be given. It is not just the 'fact' of suffering which causes anguish to the believer in God but also the 'unfairness' of it all. There are millions of people who have never known a minute free of

suffering and pain. Why does it happen? Is there some overall purpose behind it all or is life ultimately a meaningless experience?

These are questions that a believer in the Christian God cannot evade. In the end it all boils down to a dilemma which can be simply stated:

Either God does want to remove suffering but cannot - in which case he cannot be all-powerful
Or God can remove suffering but does not - in which case he cannot be all-loving.

Christianity and suffering

The Christian faith inherited most of the answers that it puts forward to suffering from Judaism. All of them are firmly rooted in the Old Testament. Amongst them are:

1] Suffering is the direct consequence of human sin in the world today. This answer is very limited. To be free people must be able to choose wrong as well as right. Sometimes people do bring suffering on themselves. Many others, though, are not suffering for their own sinful actions. Sin cannot explain, for example, the suffering of the child born with the HIV virus, blind or deaf.

2] Suffering is due to the Devil, a mighty force opposed to God. Who, though, created the Devil? If it was God why did he do it knowing the havoc that Satan would cause? This is not an explanation that would convince many today.

3] God alone knows the reason for suffering. The

BOX I

JOB 1.21

Naked I came from the womb, naked I shall return whence I came. The Lord giveth and the Lord taketh away; blessed be the name of the Lord.

BOX 2

THE CATHOLIC CATECHISM

Very often illness provokes a search for God and a return to him. [1501]

Talk it over

Do you think that suffering in the world is
a problem or a challenge to everyone -
whether they believe in God or not? How
do you understand the problem?

most well-known book about suffering is that of
Job in the Old Testament. Job was a righteous man
whose faith in God was severely tested when Satan
asked God for permission to rob Job of everything
- his riches, his friends and his health. At the end
of his long book Job finally reaches his conclusion
- that suffering is a mystery and to ask questions
about it shows a marked lack of faith in God [box
1]. Yet how can anyone witness suffering on a vast,
and indiscriminate, scale without questioning the

existence of a loving, caring and all-powerful God?

Clearly no single answer can cover the full
extent of suffering. Those who continue to believe
in God despite the vast amount of suffering that
they find in the world, and often experience for
themselves, must have compelling reasons for doing
so. The traditional Christian answer is to fall back
on faith when all attempts to understand, or
explain, fail.

[A] Natural disasters
almost always seem to
strike the defenceless,
poor and vulnerable. If
you were granted an
interview what questions
would you want to ask
God about them?

Matthew 25.31-46; John 14.1-3; 1.Corinthians 15.12-17

2:31 Death

KEY QUESTION

WHAT DO CHRISTIANS BELIEVE ABOUT DEATH AND LIFE AFTER DEATH?

Christians often speak of the 'four last things' by which they mean death, judgement, heaven and hell. They believe that the relationship that they have formed with God in this life survives death and reaches beyond the grave. All that they believe, and hope for, beyond death are based on the resurrection of Christ from the dead.

Death

At a Christian funeral service hope for the future is expressed within the context of the resurrection of Christ. As the coffin is carried into the church the priest says words from John 11.25,26: "I am the resurrection and the life; he who believes in me, though he die, yet shall he live, and whoever lives and believes in me shall never die." Throughout the service that follows Christians affirm their faith in a life beyond the grave. In the extract from the Church of England burial service [box 1] this is described as a 'sure and certain hope' and based on the precedent of the death, burial and resurrection of Jesus. Because Jesus rose from the dead so will all those who believe in him.

BOX 1

THE CHURCH OF ENGLAND BURIAL SERVICE

We have entrusted our brother/sister to God's merciful keeping, and we now commit his/her body to the ground: earth to earth, ashes to ashes, dust to dust: in sure and certain hope of the resurrection to eternal life through our Lord Jesus Christ, who died, was buried and rose again for us. To him be glory for ever and ever.

In Memory Of
A Devoted Husband and Wife
MARK AND ANN MAGGS
A Very Dear Dad and Mum
SADLY TAKEN FROM US
IN JANUARY 1994
AGED 80 AND 73 YEARS
Time passes but love and memories still remain
God bless you both
until we meet again
x x x

Judgement

The Bible teaches that people will be judged after death on the life that they have lived. The Roman Catholic Church believes in a 'particular judgement', immediately after death, when people enter heaven after purgatory or hell. There will be a 'general judgement' when Jesus returns to the earth at his Second Coming. When this happens every true believer will recognise Jesus as their Lord.

Heaven and Hell

Heaven, the destination of all true Christian believers, means enjoying the presence of God for the whole of eternity. Christians believe that Jesus, by his death and resurrection, opened up heaven for all believers. In this place there will be : "… no more death, no more grief or dying or pain. The old things have disappeared." *[Revelation 21.4]*. Hell is precisely the opposite. This is the place of eternal separation from God. Jesus spoke more than once of hell as a place of eternal torment and flames - imagery taken from Gehenna, the rubbish dump east of Jerusalem which continually burned.

Purgatory

Roman Catholics believe that, at death, no-one is fit to enter directly into heaven. A time of purification and cleansing is needed beforehand and this takes place in purgatory. Those on earth are given the responsibility of making sure that the

[A] What are the 'four last things'?

Do you think that death is the end or is there something beyond it? If so, what form do you think that this life beyond death might take?

amount of time someone spends in purgatory is as brief as possible and this they do through prayers for those who have died. You can find how a modern writer, C.S.Lewis, describes this in box 3.

Other Christians, though, believe that Jesus has made it possible for them to enter directly into heaven when they die and that no cleansing or purification is required.

BOX 2

1 CORINTHIANS 15. 13,14

If there is no resurrection from the dead, then not even Christ has been raised. And if Christ has not been raised, our preaching is useless and so is your faith.

Eternal Life

It is a strong teaching of the Christian faith that no-one who believes in Christ should be frightened of death – or what lies beyond it.

Christians believe that Jesus was God and yet he became human. After spending time on earth and being put to death he returned to heaven. Likewise, the relationship that Christians have with God cannot be broken by death. It continues because they have begun to enjoy eternal life even before they die. This eternal life begins on earth and nothing, not even death, can destroy it.

BOX 3

C.S.LEWIS. LETTERS TO MALCOLM: CHIEFLY ON PRAYER

Our souls demand Purgatory, don't they? Would it not break the heart if God said to us, 'It is true, my son, that your breath smells and your rags drip with mud and slime but we are all charitable here and no one will upbraid you with these things, nor draw away from you. Enter into the joy'. Should we not reply, 'With submission, sir, and if there is not objection, I'd rather be cleansed first.' 'It may hurt, you know.' Even so, sir'. ·

1. St Athanasius was an early Church leader. He agreed that people naturally fear death but said that those who put their faith in Jesus should despise those things that they naturally fear.
a. What do you think it is about death that people most fear?
b. How do you think that faith in Jesus might help to lessen that fear?
c. What relevance do you think this might have to the way that a Christian feels about euthanasia?

2. "Christians should not be afraid of death."
a. Do you agree?
b. What reassurances are there in Christian teaching which are designed to take away the fear of dying and death?

[B] What are Christians led to believe happens to them after they die?

3:1 | Human Rights [1]

In 1948, just after it was formed, the United Nations drew up one of its most important documents – a list of 'rights' which every human being in the world had a right to expect. The remainder of the 20th century saw a constant struggle to extend these rights to every human being but as the century ended, and another began, they remained but a distant dream for thousands of people [see box 1]. This must be a matter of deep concern for all Christians who believe that God has created all people to be equal – and that a denial of that equality is also a denial of their fundamental humanity.

[A] What should every human being have the right to expect from the government of their country?

The Charter of Human Rights

1] All human beings are born free and equal, and entitled to enjoy this freedom irrespective of their sex, race, colour, religion or age.

2] Each person should enjoy liberty and personal security.

3] No-one should be a slave under the control of someone else.

4] No-one should undergo torture, unfair arrest, detention or exile - for any reason.

5] Everyone should be treated as equal in the eyes of the law. If arrested they have a right to expect a fair, open and public trial at which they are presumed to be innocent until or unless proved guilty.

6] Everyone has the right to enjoy freedom of movement both within their own country and also freedom to travel abroad.

7] Men and women of a legal age have the right to marry and have a family - regardless of their race or religion. Once married, both men and women have the right to be treated equally..

8] Everyone has the right to own their own property. The State does not have the right to take that property away without a proper legal reason.

9] Everyone has the right to freedom of thought, opinion, conscience and religion. They also have the right to express those beliefs openly and freely.

10] Everyone has the right to meet together with other like-minded people in a 'peaceful assembly' and to join associations or unions with others if they wish.

11] Everyone has the right to take part in the government of their country, or local community, if they wish.

12] Everyone has the right to have paid employment and to receive a reasonable wage for the work that they are doing.

13] Everyone has the right to enjoy reasonable periods of leisure, working hours and paid holidays.

14] Everyone has the right to receive a reasonable level of education for themselves and for their children.

15] Everyone has the right to expect that their own reasonable needs will be met - for housing, medical care and social security when they are ill or too old to provide for themselves.

1 Look carefully at the different aspects of the United Nations Declaration on Human Rights. Take five of the rights covered by the Declaration and give examples from the modern world of instances where these rights seem to be under threat - or where they are being broken.

2 Why do you think that governments so often deny basic human rights to their citizens - what could they possibly hope to gain by doing so?

3 Can you think of any violations of human rights which have taken place in recent years?

4 Using the information given in box 1 and on this page, write a description of the work of Amnesty International.

Amnesty International

Amnesty International, formed in 1961, has tried to bring abuses of human rights out into the open. It works to:

1] Secure the abolition of the death penalty worldwide. There are still some eighty countries which retain the death penalty for crimes ranging from murder to drug trafficking.

2] The abolition of torture used to elicit information from people who have been arrested.

3] Secure a speedy, and fair, trial for all people who have been arrested.

4] The release of all 'prisoners of conscience' from prison. A prisoner of conscience is someone who has been arrested, and imprisoned, because of sincerely held religious or political beliefs – and not for committing a criminal act.

[B] Why do you think it is important that people should be able to meet with other like-minded people?

16] Everyone has the right to participate in the cultural activities of their community and to share in any scientific or economic advances that society makes.

17] Everyone has duties to their community to ensure the full recognition and respect for the rights and freedoms of others.

BOX 1

AMNESTY INTERNATIONAL LEAFLET

*Amnesty International is engaged in what is often a life or death struggle to defend human rights in many countries all over the world...
Only by becoming a mass movement for human rights can we hope to play our full part in ending the international hypocrisy which surrounds the plight of so many - those who suffer alone or collectively amidst a deafening silence to the Universal Declaration of Human Rights... Amnesty's sole reason for existence is to campaign against torture and execution and for the release of men and women imprisoned for their beliefs, colour, ethnic origin, language and religion... It is the inalienable right of people to exercise freedom of speech, association or organisation without fear...*

3:2 The Rights of Women and Children

KEY QUESTION

WHICH BASIC HUMAN RIGHTS ARE OFTEN DENIED TO WOMEN AND CHILDREN IN THE MODERN WORLD – AND WHAT IS BEING DONE ABOUT IT?

The Declaration on Human Rights [see unit 3.1] is based on the principle that everyone in the world is equal and so should be treated in the same, fair way. In this unit we look at two areas of life, involving well over 50% of the world's population, in which basic human rights are often denied:

Children's Rights

Until 1922 few people were aware that children had 'rights' but in that year the founder of the Save the Children Fund published a 'Charter on the Rights of Children' insisting that:
1] No child should be exploited by others.
2] Every child should be given the opportunity of maturing physically, intellectually and emotionally at their own pace and in their own way.
3] Each child should be taught that true happiness lies in the way of serving others.

The United Nations Declaration on the Rights of the Child, published in 1989, recognised that millions of children worldwide were living in conditions which stunted their growth. It insisted that every child should have special protection with proper levels of nutrition, housing, recreational facilities and medical care. To mature each child needs to know love, care and protection. He or she needs special protection when natural disasters strike and, in normal times, from all cruelty and neglect. They should also be kept safe from any form of discrimination based on their nationality or religion.

In the modern world we have become aware of two kinds of danger which offer acute risks to children and young people:
1] Danger from war. In many recent wars the threat to children and young people has been particularly acute. Often children, from the age of six onwards, have been drawn into the conflict and taught to carry and use weapons. In others children

---

BOX I

MARK 10.13-16

People were bringing little children to Jesus to have him touch them, but the disciples rebuked them. When Jesus saw this, he was indignant. He said to them, 'Let the little children come to me, and do not hinder them, for the kingdom of God belongs to such as these. I tell you the truth, anyone who will not receive the Kingdom of God like a little child will never enter it.' And he took the children in his arms, put his hands on them and blessed them.

▶ Work to do

1 a. Which rights of children were highlighted by the Charter published by Save the Children and that published by the United Nations in 1949?
b. Why do you think that these rights of children were denied to them for so long?

2 Describe TWO of the special dangers that confront many children in the modern world.

3 Describe TWO ways in which prejudice against women may show itself.

4 How does the Bible reflect prejudice against women?

5 For a man of his time Jesus broke down many barriers in his dealings with women. Look up the following references and make notes on them:
a. Mark 12.40.
b. Mark 10. 10,12,
c. Luke 7. 36-49.
d. John 8. 1-11.

[A] Why do you think that society has been so slow to accept that children and women have full human rights?

 Talk it over

Why do you think that basic human rights are often denied to children and women in the modern world?

BOX 2

CHURCH OF ENGLAND REPORT. CHILD ABUSE AND NEGLECT

The effects of child abuse are long lasting. Many people take years before they can begin to talk about what has happened. For many the ability to form trusting close relationships with other adults and with children is badly damaged by their childhood experiences

have seen their parents killed and been left to face the future as orphans.

2] Danger from abuse or neglect. In 1988 the Church of England published a report, 'Child abuse and neglect', which highlighted the risk to thousands of children in the UK from unwanted adult sexual attention [box 2]. It is thought that as many as 1 in 5 of adults in this country were sexually abused when they were children. The neglect of a child by its parents can be equally damaging in the long-term leading to the injury or even the death of the child.

Women's Rights

There is still a great gulf between the way that men and women are treated worldwide. Although women outnumber men [52% to 48%] they earn just 10% of the world's income and own no more than 1% of the property. In the United Kingdom it has been illegal since 1975 to discriminate against women in recruitment, promotion and training in work. It also became illegal in the same year for anyone to dismiss a woman from her work because she was pregnant. Women, though, still occupy few of the top posts in business because of the problems of combining work with family responsibilities.

Prejudice against women goes back to the Bible. In the Old Testament men had dominant roles in family and social life and this was carried over into the early Christian Church. This subservience has continued down to the present time with some Churches, notably the Roman Catholic and Orthodox Churches, refusing to ordain women into the Christian priesthood. Clearly there is a long way to go before women can be truly considered to be equal to men in all respects in society.

3:3 | War and Violence

KEY QUESTION

How has
warfare
changed in
the 20th
century and
what has
been the
consequence
of this?

Wars have always been a fact of life [boxes 1 and 2]. There is certainly no evidence to suggest that human beings are finding new, and better, ways of solving their conflicts and disagreements.

Two World Wars

During the 20th century more than 100 million people have died throughout the world as a direct result of war. During the First World War [1914-18] 95% of the casualties were soldiers but in recent years over 90% of those killed in conflicts have been civilians. In the First World War 9 million people died and over 21 million people were seriously injured. In World War 11 there were 55 million deaths of which 16 million were soldiers and 39 million were civilians. Modern weapons and the way that wars are now fought forces civilians in the battle-field to pay a much higher price than professional soldiers.

Wars of different kinds

Since the Second World War ended in 1945 there have been more than 270 wars in different parts of the world. Technically, a war is any conflict which lasts longer than 60 minutes and in which regular forces from at least one side are involved. These conflicts fall into two groups:
1] Conflicts between nations. Since 1945 there have been wars in the Middle East and in South East Asia – including the Korean War [1950-53]; the Vietnam War [1965-73]; the Iran/Iraq conflict [1980-88] and the Gulf War [1991].
2] Civil wars and 'wars of liberation'. A 'civil war' is a conflict within the borders of one country in which the government is involved in fighting its fellow-countrymen. When the two main tribes in Rwanda were involved in a civil war in 1994 it is estimated that 1 million people from the largest tribe alone were slaughtered.

The cost of war

The cost of any war must be measured in terms of:
1] Destruction. The number of people killed and injured, the destruction of towns and countryside and the number of families whose lives have been shattered all need to be taken into account when assessing the cost of a war. When the Allied Forces, led by the USA and Britain, opposed Saddam Hussein in the Gulf in 1991 the cost of the conflict was estimated at £55 million excluding the cost of rebuilding a devastated country which began when the war ended.
2] Refugees. War forces thousands of people to leave their homes and, often, their country as well. Usually these people are unable, or too frightened, to return home. This turns them into refugees i.e. people without a home. Today there are thought to be as many as 17 million refugees in the world including many who have been without a permanent home since the 1950s. Almost all of the world's refugees were created by war or conflict.
3] Economic cost. War inevitably destroys homes, crops, water and power supplies, industry, hospitals and schools. All of these vital services have to be replaced when the war is over. This uses up vast amounts of money - money and resources that poor countries can ill afford. The developing countries of the world [see unit 3.7] spend twenty

Why do you think that the Arms Race is a particularly disturbing aspect of life in the world today?

1 a. List some statistics which indicate the toll that warfare has had on human life in the 20th century.
b. How has the nature of warfare changed as the 20th century has developed?

2 What is a war?

3 List TWO different types of conflict and write TWO sentences about each of them.

4 Describe THREE effects that war is likely to have on the different countries fighting.

times more on buying military weapons than they do on feeding and helping their poorest citizens [see box 3]. The need to constantly update weapons is called 'the Arms Race'.

More about nuclear weapons, and the threat that they present, in unit 3.4. Here the simple point is made that nuclear weapons have only been used twice in actual warfare - with the dropping of two atomic bombs on the Japanese cities of Hiroshima and Nagazaki in 1945. The use of these two bombs brought the Second World War to an end. In size and scope they were tiny compared to modern nuclear weapons but they still killed more than

140,000 people in the two cities. Thousands more suffered from the permanent, and appaling, after-effects of radiation.

[A] The victims of war. Do you think that anyone really 'wins' in a war?

3:4 | Nuclear War

The first atomic bombs were developed by the USA during the Second World War and dropped for the first, and only, time in anger on the Japanese cities of Hiroshima and Nagazaki in 1945.

The Nuclear Club

When the first bombs were dropped only the USA had the capacity to manufacture atomic weapons. It was not long, however, before other countries developed the raw materials, and the necessary technology, to join the 'Nuclear Club'. The basic ingredient needed to make a nuclear bomb is plutonium and this is produced by nuclear reactors.

Soon the 'Nuclear Club' expanded. In 1949 the USSR developed, and tested, its own nuclear weapons. A 'Nuclear Arms Race' soon grew up between the USA and the USSR as they competed against each other to produce bigger, better, and more powerful, nuclear weapons. Within a few years this Club had five members – France, the UK and China joining the USA and the USSR. The modern 'Nuclear Club', though, is now much larger and thought to include Israel, Pakistan, India, South Africa, Iran and North Korea among other countries. Many other countries are also believed to have the potential to make nuclear weapons in the early years of the 21st century. The attempt to contain the expansion of nuclear weapons has failed and the whole world must live with any future consequences. .

The Balance of Terror

Although there have been over 270 wars since the Second World War ended they have all been fought locally. None of them thankfully has developed into a worldwide conflict. Some people argue that this has been because of the 'Balance of Terror' which stops one country using nuclear weapons

BOX 1

PACEM IN TERRIS, ROMAN CATHOLIC DOCUMENT, 1965

The monstrous power of nuclear weapons will have fatal consequences for life on earth. Justice, right reason and humanity therefore urgently demand that the arms race should cease....nuclear weapons should be banned.

Look at the quotation in box 2. Do you think we have realised the potential destructive force of nuclear weapons.

1 What is the 'Nuclear Club'?

2 a. What is the 'Balance of Terror'?
b. Why do some people argue that the 'Balance of Terror' has kept peace in the world since the end of the Second World War? c. Do you feel comfortable living in a world where the peace is only kept by the balance of weapons held by different countries? Explain the reasons for the answer that you have given.

3 What are the arguments for and against the belief that nuclear weapons act as a deterrent in the modern world?

[A] How do you think Nuclear weapons have altered the way we look at life and death

because of the fear of what other countries could do to them in retaliation. Others, though, are not so sure pointing out that the world has almost suffered a nuclear catastrophe on at least one known occasion - during the Cuban Missile Crisis in the early 1960s and probably on other occasions as well. The 'Balance of Terror' seems a very flimsy foundation on which to base world peace.

The deterrent argument

1] NUCLEAR WEAPONS - A DETERRENT
The debate about nuclear weapons revolves around whether they act as a genuine deterrent or not. Those who believe they do point out that:
a. It seems to work - there has been no major war in Europe since 1945.
b. The possession of nuclear weapons is bound to deter others - because of the immense cost of using such weapons against a country that also possesses them.
c. Nuclear weapons give a country a bargaining chip - they can give up their weapons if other sides agree to do so

2] NUCLEAR WEAPONS - NOT A DETERRENT
a. The growth of nuclear weapons, and the number of countries now possessing them, makes war more, not less, likely.
b. The use of such weapons could not be justified under any circumstances - other countries know this and so the deterrent argument does not hold.
c. The vast amounts of money spent on nuclear weapons could far better be used in alleviating poverty, illiteracy and bad housing throughout the world.
d. Although some steps have been taken towards disarmament these steps are small and there is no indication that nuclear countries really want to move towards disarmament. That makes the world a very dangerous place.

Disarmament

It is clear that the world does not need its vast arsenals of nuclear weapons. Enough nuclear weapons now exist to destroy the world many times over. Everyone agrees that disarmament is essential. There are two possible approaches to disarmament:

1] Unilateral disarmament. This calls for one side to disarm in the belief that other sides would then be persuaded to do the same. The Roman Catholic Church argued in 'Gaudium et Spes [1965] that there should be a total ban on nuclear weapons and multilateral disarmament. A Church of England Report suggested that Britain tread this path in 1982 but the Church itself rejected it.

2] Multilateral disarmament. This looks to all sides to begin to disarm at the same rate. Although there have been a few signs of this happening the progress along this route to disarmament is going to be long and tortuous - if it happens at all.

BOX 2

ARTHUR KOESTLER, AUTHOR

Before the bomb, man had to live with the idea of his death as an individual; from now onwards, mankind has to live with the idea of death as a species.

3:5 | Pacifism

For the first three centuries of its existence few members of the Christian Church joined the Roman Army. They knew only too well the teaching of Jesus – see boxes 1 and 2 for examples. Then, when emperor Constantine became a Christian at the start of the 4th century, Christians felt free to join the army. Suddenly pacifism went out of fashion and the teaching of Jesus was forgotten. Since then it has never been the 'official' teaching of the Church and the Quakers [see below] has been the only Christian denomination committed to pacifism. This is surprising since the approach of non-violence would seem to have a secure foundation in the teaching of Jesus.

Christian pacifism

Not all pacifists are Christians. Many non-Christians believe that it is wrong to use violence or to take human life in any situation. Christians who are pacifists justify their belief on Biblical grounds:

1] The commandment 'You shall not kill' [Exodus 20.13]. This condemnation of killing would seem to be all-embracing.

2] The teachings of Jesus gathered together into the so-called Sermon on the Mount [Matthew 5-7]. Amongst the many references suggesting a pacifist approach to life are:

- 'Do not resist those who wrong you…' [5.39]
- 'Love your enemies and pray for your persecutors' [5.44]
- 'There must be no limit to your goodness…' [5.48]

It is difficult to see how killing and maiming others, even in a war, could be squared with these comments of Jesus.

3] The actions of Jesus. When Jesus was arrested [Luke 22. 39-53] by a group of soldiers led by one of his disciples, Judas, Jesus was horrified when one of his disciples, Peter, drew a sword and attempted to defend him. Jesus made it clear that violent resistance, even under extreme provocation, was not his chosen way: "Put your sword back in its place… for all who draw the sword will die by the sword. Do you not think that I can call on my Father, and he will at once put at my disposal more than twelve legions of angels?" [Matthew 26. 52-53]. Jesus later forgave those who crucified him: "Father, forgive them, for they do not know what they are doing." [Luke 23.34]. Jesus taught that forgiveness should be offered to those who wrong us time and time again [Matthew 18. 21-35].

The Society of Friends

The only branch of the Christian Church expressly committed to pacifism is the Society of Friends, the Quakers. Founded in 1652 under the leadership of George Fox they have been

[A] Why do you think that many people in society are strongly opposed to pacifism?

Talk it over

Do you think that it is realistic, in the modern world, to adopt a pacifist point of view?

Work to do

1 a. What is pacifism?
b. Explain why some Christians would refuse to fight in a war.

2 "Jesus didn't teach anything about pacifism." Do you agree with this assessment?

3 Describe the Christian and biblical teaching on which a pacifist approach to life is based.

4 a. How did Jesus react when he was arrested?
b. How might Christians follow this example and react when confronted by the violence of others?

committed to peace and reconciliation in the world ever since. In 1660 they handed over a Declaration to King Charles II in which they made their commitment to pacifism very clear [box 3]. This Declaration spelt out the Quaker belief that there was no conceivable situation in which the use of violence could be justified. Quakers argue that the only way to secure peace is to appeal to that of God which is in every person. War destroys all that is beautiful in the world. God alone can bring his love and care into every violent situation, potential and actual, in the world.

Pacifism on the front line

In times of war many pacifists register as 'conscientious objectors'. This means that they cannot, in all conscience, take up weapons and fight but it is not an easy option to take. They are likely to meet the antagonism of others who see them as traitors – or cowards. The Roman Catholic Church, which does not have a strong tradition of pacifism, teaches that those who cannot fight must offer themselves for other war duties instead. Many conscientious objectors, in the First and Second World Wars, found themselves doing such duties as

BOX 2

MATTHEW 5.39

Do not resist those who wrong you. If anyone slaps you on the right cheek, turn and offer him the other also.

BOX 3

QUAKER DECLARATION GIVEN TO KING CHARLES 11. 1660

We utterly deny all outward wars and strife; and fightings with outward weapons, for any end, or under any pretence whatever; this is our testimony to the whole world. The Spirit of Christ by which we are guided is not changeable, so at once to command us from a thing as evil, and again to move unto it; and we certainly know, and testify to the world that the Spirit of Christ, which leads us into all truth, will never move us to fight and war against any man with outward weapons, neither for the Kingdom of Christ, nor for the kingdoms of this world.

ambulance driving and stretcher carrying – tasks which placed them in the front line with all its dangers.

3:6 Just and Holy Wars

The Quakers, as we say in unit 3.5, have always been heavily committed to pacifism. Other Churches, though, have preferred to argue that certain wars, fought in the name of God and justice, have carried the seal of divine approval.

Holy Wars

The idea of a 'holy war', carried out with the authority of God, is prominent in the Old Testament. The Israelites had to battle their way into the Promised Land, the country that they believed God had given to them. This is the country now known as Israel. Battles were fought in the name of God [box 1]. Centuries later Christian armies, about to wage war in Israel against 'pagans' [Muslims] were told by Pope Urban 11 in 1095 that:

1] They were fighting for a holy and noble cause - to free Christian holy places from the Muslims.

2] They were being led into battle by God.

3] Since God was on their side so everyone opposing them were God's enemies.

4] Just as the Israelites had destroyed everything belonging to their captured enemies so they were to do likewise [box 3].

Holy Wars were wars of aggression and that made them different from Just Wars which were intended to be mainly defensive.

BOX 1

EXODUS 15. 1-4

I will sing to the Lord, for he has risen in triumph; horse and rider he has hurled into the sea... The Lord is a warrior; the Lord is his name... Pharoah's chariots and his army he has hurled into the sea. The best of Pharoah's officers are drowned in the Red Sea.

Just Wars

The Just War theory is based on the belief that whilst war is never 'right' it might, in certain situations, be justified. To be justified it must be fought by certain 'rules' which are designed to keep its destructive affects down to a minimum. In 1250 CE the Dominican friar, St Thomas Aquinas, laid down just what those 'rules' should be:

1] The war must have a 'just' cause. In practice, this means that a war can only be justified if a country is attacked - and needs to defend itself.

2] Every other possible solution to the problem has been tried, such as negotiation, without success.

3] The war must have a clear aim which is known to those directing the war. Simple vengeance against a country which has wronged another is not a justifiable aim ['to teach them a lesson']. Once the stated aim of the war has been reached the fighting must stop.

4] The war must be fought in a 'just' way. This means that:

• certain weapons of great destruction must not be used.

• only as much force can be used as is necessary to bring about a victory. Excessive force, and destruction, is ruled out. To use the language of Aquinas the force used must be 'proportionate' to the situation.

• no violence must be directed specifically against civilians.

There are three grounds in the Bible on which the idea of the Just War is based:

a. The frequent reference in the Old Testament to the wars fought by the Israelites on which the blessing of God rested. To take one example - when the Israelites escaped from Egyptian slavery, and the Egyptian army was drowned by God in the waters of the Red Sea, God was hailed as the great 'warrior' [box 1]. It was God who destroyed 'Pharoah's chariots and his army'. The cause of the Israelites was just - the land had been given to them by God.

b. Paul's advice to the Christians in Rome that they should always obey their governing authorities - because these authorities had been

1 a. What is a Just War?
b. What is a Holy War?
c. What is the difference between a Just War and a Holy War?
d. Describe THREE conditions for a Just War?

2 Explain THREE reasons which might be put forward from the Bible to justify the idea of a Just War.

given their authority to rule by God himself [box 2]. If the government of a country demands that people fight then all, including Christians, must respond.

c. The only occasion on which Jesus acted violently - when he overturned the tables of the money-changers in the Temple [Mark 11. 15-16]. The violence of Jesus was justified because he had a just cause - and the same reason can be put forward to justify certain wars.

When the 'rules' of the Just War were put forward in the 13th century war was very different to modern warfare. Even then it was felt necessary to contain war within limits - and this could be done. Such a hope, though, is wholly unrealistic today. Modern warfare kills far more civilians than soldiers although this is expressly ruled out in a Just War.

Of the many wars fought in the 20th century it would be impossible to argue that any more than a small handful could possibly have been called 'just' - and even in those the extent of the fighting went far beyond anything allowed for in the Just War theory.

BOX 2

ROMANS 13.1-5

Everyone must submit to the governing authorities... The authorities that exist have been established by God. Consequently he who rebels against the authority is rebelling against what God has established... Therefore, it is necessary to submit to the authorities...

BOX 3

RAYMOND OF ARGILES ON THE CAPTURE OF JERUSALEM.1187

In the temple and the porch of Solomon, men rode in blood up to their knees and bridle reins... the city was filled with corpses and blood.

[A] Christian armies in the past have ridden into battle behind the banner of the cross. Why do you think that most Christians today feel extremely unhappy about this?

3:7 | Developed and Developing Countries

KEY QUESTION

WHAT DO WE MEAN WHEN WE TALK OF THE DEVELOPED AND DEVELOPING COUNTRIES AND WHAT ARE THE MAIN DIFFERENCES BETWEEN THEM?

[A] Why could the future of these children be very bleak?

We live today in a divided world - one divided by wealth on the one hand and poverty on the other:

1] The north [developed world] consists of those countries which have a high standard of living and includes North America, Western Europe and Australasia. 25% of the world's population lives in the Developed World but these countries consume 80% of the world's resources - energy, food etc.

2] The south [developing world] consists of those countries which have a very low standard of living including South America, Africa and India. These countries, with 75% of the world's population, live off just 20% of the world's resources.

Developing countries

The countries of the Developing World share:
1] A high level of malnutrition. The world produces enough grain for every man, woman and child to eat 3,000 calories a day - more than

BOX I

MARK 10.23-28

Jesus looked round and said to his disciples, 'How hard it will be for those who have riches to enter the kingdom of God!' And the disciples were amazed at his words. But Jesus said to them again,'Children, how hard it is to enter the kingdom of God. It is easier for a camel to go through the eye of a needle than for a rich man to enter the kingdom of God.

enough for a healthy life. 600 million people in the world, though, live in absolute poverty. The Brandt Report [see box 2] reported that just 1.5% of a single year's world expenditure on arms would provide all the farming equipment needed to make each Developing Country self-sufficient in food production.

2] A largely illiterate population. There is a direct link between poverty and levels of literacy. It is almost impossible for illiterate people, about 1,000 million of them, to find their way out of poverty.

3] Lack of clean drinking water. 25 million people die each year from water-borne diseases. 2.4 billion [2,400 million] people do not have adequate sanitation - with all the problems that this causes for health. 2 billion [1 in every 3] people in the world do not have access to a clean water supply.

4] Poor medical care. Inadequate food and the lack of clean water inevitably lead to severe health problems. Babies and the elderly are the most vulnerable. 20 million

1 When we talk of living in a divided world what do we mean?

2 List FOUR differences between the developed and the developing countries of the world.

3 Describe THREE characteristics of a developing country.

Clearly we live in a divided world. Do you think there is any chance of the world's wealth being distributed more fairly during your life-time? If so, how do you think it might be brought about?

people die from malnutrition each year and 3 out of every 4 of these never see their fifth birthday. People in developing countries lack many facilities that are taken for granted elsewhere – access to hospital, doctors and dentists; immunisation programmes against common killer diseases such as malaria; prenatal and antenatal care and education in basic hygiene. Poor medical facilities inevitably lead to a low life expectancy. In the UK males can reasonably hope to reach the age of 75 and women 78. In many developing countries, however, the life expectancy of both men and women is barely 50 years. With comparatively few people reaching old age a high proportion of people in these countries are under the age of fifteen.

5] Most people work in agriculture – 3 out of every 4 men in many countries. This can be compared with a figure of just 4% in Britain. Farming in the developing world is largely one of subsistence – where people only grow just enough for their own needs without having any left over to sell to others[see box 2]. This means that they have no money to buy other essential goods.

The Brandt Report

Although the Brandt Report ['North-South. A Programme for Survival'] was published in 1980 it is still the most complete study of world poverty. Depressingly the situation has not improved in the last 20 years – if anything it has deteriorated. The Report described a world divided firmly into two parts – the North [the 'haves'] and the South [the 'have-nots']. Brandt pointed out that in the poor South the birth-rate is high whilst the life expectancy is low. In a world in which parents depend on their children to support them when they grow old they will continue to have many children as an 'insurance policy' against future poverty.

Yet, as Brandt pointed out, the economies of

countries in the North and South are heavily dependent on each other. Everyone, rich and poor, shares the same planet. What happens on one side of the globe drastically affects those on the other. The rich countries not only have a moral duty to support the poorer countries but it is actually in their long-term interests to do so.

[B] Describe three characteristics of this poor family not shared by its equivalent in the rich Northern countries.

BOX 2

THE BRANDT REPORT

Many hundreds of millions of people in the poorer countries are preoccupied solely with survival and elementary needs. For them work is frequently not available or, when it is, pay is very low and conditions often barely tolerable. Homes are constructed of impermeable [non-waterproof] materials and have neither piped water nor sanitation. Electricity is a luxury... Primary schools, where they exist, may be free and not too far away, but children are needed for work and cannot easily be spared for schooling... Flood, drought or disease affecting people or livestock can destroy livelihoods without hope of compensation.

3:8   World Hunger

Talk it over

Do you think that all people have the 'right' to enjoy what they need from the earth's resources and, if so, where does that leave people who are deprived of these resources today?

KEY QUESTION

WHY IS THERE SO MUCH HUNGER, AND MALNUTRITION, IN THE WORLD?

[A] Why do you think that rich countries can produce all the food they need but not the poorer countries?

More people in to-day's world die from malnutrition [hunger] than from any other cause, including war. The problem of world hunger is far more to do with greed, politics, economics and power than it is to do with an actual shortage of food. In the modern world malnutrition kills:

- 1 person every 2.5 seconds,
- 24 people every minute,
- 35,000 people every day,
- 20 million people every year.

75% of those who die from malnutrition are under the age of five.

Understanding world hunger

World hunger has been much misunderstood and four important points about it need to be underlined:

1] There are not too many mouths to feed in the world. It is true that the population in many countries of the world is increasing rapidly [see unit 3.10]. It is also true that those countries in which the population is increasing most rapidly are the countries with the greatest food problems. Yet these same countries have a low population density - in Africa 18 people live to a square kilometre compared with 96 people in Western Europe. The problem is that in many developing countries the land is a very poor quality - or infertile. These countries cannot afford to improve the quality of their land and so the crop yield is very low.

2] There is enough food to go round. There is plenty of food in the world - more than enough to feed the present population of over 6 million. In fact, each year vast amounts of food are destroyed in many countries because of over production. The simple problem is that most of the food is in the wrong place - so the USA with just 6% of the world's population consumes, and wastes, 30% of the world's food supply.

3] Natural disasters, such as floods or earthquakes, usually occur in the world's poorest areas. People in these areas often build in vulnerable places where deforestation has taken place and the natural

BOX I

SECOND VATICAN COUNCIL OF THE ROMAN CATHOLIC CHURCH

God destined the earth and all it contains for all peoples... Therefore every man has the right to possess a sufficient amount of the earth's goods for himself and his family... When a person is in extreme necessity he has the right to supply himself with what he needs out of the riches of others.

[B] A Harvest Festival service. Do you think it hypocritical if the rich countries thank God for his provision whilst other countries go without the basics of life?

disaster has a devastating effect. When a natural disaster happens in wealthy countries the equipment, the transport and the man-power, exists to minimise its effects considerably.

4] Scientists cannot cure the world's shortage of food. Attempts to do this have failed. In the 1960s and the 1970s hope was expressed of developing new, higher-yielding strains of wheat and rice but no-one speaks in those terms today.

The politics of food

Speaking on television some years ago Susan George, the economist, put the world shortage of food in perspective. She pointed out that:

• There are 3,500 calories to every kilo of grain so a ton of grain supplies 3.5 million calories.

• The Food and Agricultural Organisation at the United Nations says that 2,300 calories intake each day is adequate for each person to have proper nutrition.

• The minimum yearly intake for a healthy life is 839,500 calories. A ton of grain provides this for four people.

• A million tons would feed more than 4 million people. To cover all the people who now die from malnutrition in a year would take just 5 million tons of grain altogether.

BOX 2

BASIL HUME, LATE ROMAN CATHOLIC CARDINAL

There is surely a moral imperative to bring sanity to this crazy and deadly situation, to restore human dignity, to promote development and the possibility of peace. We must look at ourselves and our lifestyles. We must examine and change the processes and structures of the world which at the moment promote division and ultimately bring death...

 Work to do

1 a. In box 2 Cardinal Hume described the situation in the world today over resources as being 'deadly and crazy'. What do you think he was particularly referring to?
b. Do you agree that millions of people in to-day's world lack human dignity because of their situation and needs? If so, what do you think could be done to restore that human dignity?

2 What would you say to the person who maintains that there is simply not enough food to go round in today's world?

3 How would you answer the person who maintains that poor countries only have themselves to blame for hunger because they have not tackled their population problems?

3:9 | Cafod

There are many Christian charities which work amongst the poor and the needy in to-day's world. One such organisation is CAFOD - the Catholic Fund for Overseas Development. It was set up by Catholic bishops in 1962 to assist the poor and disadvantaged throughout the world to help themselves. Projects financed by CAFOD attempt to tackle the causes, as well as the symptoms, of disease, ignorance and poverty. The goal of the organisation is to: "Promote human development and social justice in witness to the Christian faith and Gospel values."

To this end CAFOD now supports well over 500 different projects in more than 75 countries. The Irish equivalent of CAFOD is TROCAIRE ['Mercy'] and the two organisations often work alongside each other in their projects.

Tackling world development

CAFOD sets out to tackle the most pressing issues in world development by working along three interconnected lines:

1] Raising funds To bring home the link between the money raised and the needs that it helps to meet special sponsored fasts are held by CAFOD during Lent and October each year. These special days, a unique feature of the work of this charity, encourage churches and individuals to go without food for a day and to give the money raised to CAFOD projects throughout the world. Each year more than £20 million is raised to help the poor and disadvantaged. It also underlines the belief that the task of alleviating poverty is a spiritual as well as a physical undertaking. For centuries fasting has been a spiritual activity encouraged by the Catholic Church.

2] To send aid Aid comes in two, but equally important, ways:

a. Short-term aid. CAFOD carries a fund which can respond quickly when a natural disaster strikes or when a situation, such as the recent wars in Bosnia and Kosovo, creates many refugees. The organisation is able to gather food, medicines and shelter together so that it can respond to the need rapidly. Often a number of charities in Britain such as CAFOD, Christian Aid and Oxfam launch a joint appeal to the public for money when the need is particularly acute.

b. Long-term aid. Caritas is an international Catholic organisation which works on the ground in many needy countries. Much of the money raised by CAFOD is channelled through Caritas into various long-term projects associated with such areas of need as health care, irrigation and food production projects, education both amongst children and adults etc. Health workers take care and education to

---

BOX 1

POPE JOHN PAUL II, SPEAKING IN LIVERPOOL. 1982

I hope that, despite all the obstacles, the generosity of your hearts will never weaken. I hope that through programmes such as the Catholic Fund for Overseas Development, you will continue to help the poor, to feed the hungry and to contribute to the cause of development. Always keep alive your Gospel tradition.

BOX 2

THE CATECHISM OF THE CATHOLIC CHURCH [1932]

The duty of making oneself a neighbour to others and actively serving them becomes even more urgent when it involves the disadvantaged, in whatever area this might be. 'As you did it to one of the least of these my brethren, you did it to me.'

1 What was CAFOD set up to achieve and how does it set about reaching its objectives?

2 Explain how the work of CAFOD/ TROCAIRE helps those people in to-day's world who are in the greatest need.

3 Describe THREE ways in which CAFOD helps people in developing countries.

4 What is there in the life and teaching of Jesus to encourage Christians to support the work of organisations like CAFOD?

farmers and others who have no fixed home. In countries such as Brazil there are thousands of children living on the streets of most large cities with no homes. CAFOD supports workers who take education and other kinds of help to these children.

3] Education The educating of people at home about development issues is a very important part of the work of CAFOD. 5p in every pound raised by the organisation is spent on educating Catholics in Britain, mainly through churches and schools, about the needs of developing countries. CAFOD workers go into schools to speak to classes, and assemblies, about various overseas projects and the organisation also produces resource material for teachers to use.

Why get involved?

The struggle for equality and justice in the many poor parts of the world is one that should engage the hearts and minds of Christians, including Roman Catholics, everywhere. Following the example of Jesus they believe that the love of God needs to be taken everywhere [see unit 3.11]. There is enough teaching in the Gospels about justice and treating people with care and compassion to show that this is an essential part of the Christian Gospel. Christians are called to work with God to create a world which is less self-centred and selfish. If the Christian Gospel is what it claims to be then it is more than just a personal way to salvation - it is the means by which God's purpose for equality and justice will be brought about for the whole world.

[A] In what kind of situations might short term aid be needed?

3:10 | World Population

KEY QUESTION

**WHAT IS
HAPPENING
TO THE
POPULATION OF
THE WORLD?**

One of the greatest threats to the future of the human race in the 21st century is the uncontrolled growth of world population. Put simply:

- more than one baby is born every second,
- 200,000 babies – the equivalent of a small city – are born every day,
- the population of the world doubles every 35 years.

The total population of the world is now over 6 billion people. This compares with two billion in 1930 and 3.5 billion as recently as 1970.

In most Western countries the population is relatively stable. In recent years Norway, Sweden and Switzerland have actually expressed concerned that their populations are falling. In the United Kingdom the total population increased modestly from 56 million in 1971 to 59.4 million in 2000. It is expected that this will rise to 62.2 billion by 2021. In developing countries, though, the growth is much faster. In Kenya, for example, it is increasing by 8% each year whilst 1 in every 4 people in the modern world are Chinese – a total population of more than 1.5 billion.

The problems of world population

This 'population explosion' has caused many social problems:

1] A shortage of suitable. housing. Across the world millions of people live in temporary and totally unsuitable accommodation. Much of the housing that exists lacks many of the basic amenities. It is estimated that 3 million new houses will be needed in Britain by the year 2025, a need brought about largely by the growth of single-parent families caused by the increase in the divorce rate.

2] A growth in large cities. About 50% of the

▶ **Work to do**

1 What has happened to the population of the world during the 20th century?

2 Write TWO sentences about each of the following in the context of the world's expanding population:

a. Housing.

b. The growth of large cities.

c. Human waste.

3 How is the problem of world population growth likely to be solved in the future?

world's population now lives in a city. People who have tried in the past to scrape a living through subsistence farming have been forced to move into cities to find work. In 1935 there were just 56 cities in the world with a population of more than one million. By 1960 this figure had increase to 100 and there are now over 500. Mexico City is the world's largest city with a population of well over 15 million. The growth of large cities causes many problems. The larger the city the higher the level of pollution. Cities are built on valuable green land that can never be replaced. Cities also generate social problems of their own including violence and crime, alcoholism and the abuse of drugs. Suitable housing cannot be provided and cities spawn slums, shanty towns and homelessness.

3] An increase in the amount of human waste. Most of the pollution of the world's rivers, streams, oceans and air comes from industrialised, city life.

Many attempts have been made in the latter part of the 20th century to slow down population

---

BOX 1

SUSAN GEORGE. HOW THE OTHER HALF DIES

When there is only a 50-50 chance of your children living past five years, you've got to plan to have many children. And when there is no social security, or health insurance, who else is going to look after you if not your children? If we looked at life from the point of view of those who say 'my children are my only wealth' would we still be so keen on birth control... The poor of the world will start using contraceptive devices very quickly indeed, just as soon as real development and a fairer deal in life lets them do so.

[A] What do you think could be done in developing countries to make sure that more children survive infancy - and how could this bring about a drop in the number of babies born?

---

growth but these have largely failed. The two countries with the largest growing populations, China and India, have tried to bribe, persuade or compel people to limit the size of their families but these attempts have made little lasting impression. Clearly much of the solution lies with a more effective distribution and education about birth-control. Attempts to do this are not helped by the attitude of the Roman Catholic Church and its teaching that all forms of unnatural birth-control are against the will of God. This problem is most acute in the countries of South America where the Roman Catholic Church has enormous influence and the growth in population is very rapid. It is interesting that:

a. The majority of Roman Catholics in Western countries like the USA and the UK ignore this aspect of the Church's social teaching. In the UK, for instance, it is estimated that over 80% of Roman Catholic couples do not follow the Church's teaching on contraception.

b. In South American countries many priests teach that the problem of poverty can only be solved by a redistribution of wealth to the poor - and not by artificial attempts to limit the size of families.

To be successful the problem of over population must be tackled along several fronts - by lowering infant mortality rates; increasing the level of literacy and education; raising the status and education of women; spreading wealth more equally throughout the world and making free and ready access to contraceptives available to everyone.

3:11 | The Christian Response

KEY QUESTION

**WHAT DID
JESUS HAVE
TO SAY ABOUT
POVERTY
AND THE
DISTRIBUTION
OF WEALTH?**

In the Old Testament and New Testament the uneven distribution of wealth was a constant theme. It was strongly believed that the resources of the earth were provided by God – for everyone to enjoy.

The prophets and Jesus

The prophets in the Old Testament delivered a strong message against the gap between rich and poor in Israelite society. The strongest message came from the prophet Amos who attacked the refusal of those with wealth to feed the poor and hungry in their community. He spoke of a plumbline being held against a wall – a standard of righteousness [uprightness] by which the nation would be judged. He made it clear that God would not accept the worship of those who went through the motions of religious worship whilst refusing to meet the real needs of the poor.

Jesus continued the prophetic denunciation of those who hoarded their wealth. Looking at his disciples on one occasion he told them: "Blessed are you who are poor, for yours is the kingdom of God. Blessed are you who hunger now, for you will be satisfied." [Luke 6.20,21]. He said that rich people who were wealthy would find that their wealth was a great obstacle which came between them and entering God's kingdom [see box 1]. Only those who shared their wealth with the poor and hungry can expect to be given a place in God's kingdom [Matthew 25. 31-46].

Building better barns

On one occasion Jesus was approached by a man who wanted him to tell his brother to share his possessions with other members of his family [Luke 12.13-21]. Jesus told him a story [parable] to illustrate the truth that the value of a man's life has little to do with the amount of possessions he has.

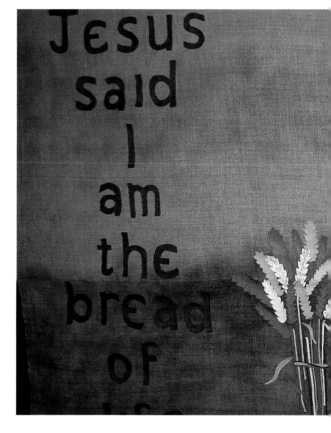

[A] Why do you think that Jesus was so keen to point out that people neglected the spiritual in their lives at their peril?

One year the ground of a rich farmer was particularly fertile and yielded a bumper crop. This overwhelmed the farmer who realised that he had nowhere to store the grain. He decided to build new barns so that the crop could be his guarantee of a future life of plenty. Jesus pointed out how short-sighted this attitude was. God demands much

BOX I

LUKE 18.22

You still lack one thing. Sell everything that you have and give to the poor, and you will have treasure in heaven. Then come, follow me.

BOX 3

JAMES 5.1-3

Now listen, you rich people, weep and wail because of the misery that is coming on you. Your wealth has rotted, and moths have eaten your clothes. Your gold and silver are corroded.

1 What message of the prophets in the Old Testament about wealth and poverty was taken up by Jesus?

2 Jesus told TWO parables about the dangers of wealth:
a. The farmer who has a bumper harvest.
b. The rich man and Lazarus. Tell each of these stories in your own words and point out the lessons that Jesus wanted his hearers to learn from them.

3 How did the early Christians try to put the teachings of Jesus about meeting the needs of the poor into practice?

The rich man died and went into the underworld from where he envied the life of Lazarus in heaven. It was too late, though, for his situation to be changed or for his relatives to be warned of the dangers of living such a selfish existence.

The early Christians

After the ascension of Jesus into heaven the early Christians sought to put his teachings into practice. In the early days of the Church we are told that they were 'one in heart and mind'. In the Christian community no-one claimed that his or her human possessions were their own but they used them all for the benefit of the whole community. We know that this community was made up of both rich and poor but together they witnessed to the resurrection of Jesus and God's grace was on all of them [Acts 4. 33]. The rich sold their land and brought the proceeds to the apostles so that the money could be used to help those in need. As a result 'there were no needy persons among them.'

Selling one's possessions and giving to the poor was an action that Jesus, and the disciples, commended highly. One of the disciples, James, spoke in very strong terms about those who had wealth but clung on to it to the very end [see box 2]. The immense needs of the world for food, education, shelter and health can only be met if there is a considerable shift of resources from the rich to the poor. The teachings of Jesus suggest that his followers should set an example by living a simple lifestyle and sharing with those in need.

more of those who have more than their fair share of the earth's resources. He said to the man: "You fool! This night your life will be demanded of you. Then who will get what you have prepared for yourself?" [12.20].

The rich man and Lazarus

Jesus told another story to illustrate his teaching that it is the poor and not the rich who will enter God's kingdom. There was a rich man who dressed in purple and fine linen and lived a life of luxury every day [Luke 16. 19-31]. A poor beggar, Lazarus, was covered in sores and lay outside the rich man's door. The beggar would have been satisfied with eating the crumbs that fell from the rich man's table but he was given nothing. Eventually the poor beggar died and was carried up into heaven.

BOX 3

LUKE 12.22-28

I tell you, do not worry about your life, what you will eat; or about your body, what you will wear. Life is more than food and the body more than clothes. Consider the ravens: they do not sow or reap, they have no storeroom or barn; yet God feeds them. And how much more valuable you are than the birds! Consider how the lilies grow. They do not labour or spin. Yet I tell you not even Solomon in all his glory was dressed like one of these. If that is how God clothes the grass of the field… how much more will he clothe you?

3:12 | God's World

HUW! YAY!

The Bible teaches that God created the universe in the beginning. He gave the responsibility of looking after his handiwork to human beings. These two themes run through the Bible from its opening chapters in the book of Genesis with the well-known account of the creation of the world [chapters 1–3].

A Divine Creation

The idea of the creative activity of God in the world is particularly strong in some of the Psalms of the Old Testament where it is given a poetic expression [see boxes 1 and 2]. In Psalm 8, for example, the writer expresses his own sense of human frailty and smallness when he looks up at the heavens, the moon and the stars above him. He then turns to God and finds that human beings, as the highest expression of God's creative activity, have been given power and authority over

everything that exists. Little wonder, then, that a note of wonder creeps into his voice when he concludes: "You make him [man] master over all that you have made…" [Psalm 8.6].

This kind of authority has always been open to all kinds of human abuse. The human race has a long history of abusing nature. Desmond Morris, a leading anthropologist in the 1970s and 1980s, blamed this Biblical idea for many of the ecological disasters of the 20th century. He said: "Who is to blame for the ecological disaster that we face? First and foremost, I accuse the religious leaders of the world. They have fed mankind with the dangerous myth that mankind is somehow above nature, and that it is our God-given right to hold dominion over the earth and subdue it… they are a disgrace."

It is the word 'authority' which has caused so much difficulty in the past – and continues to do so today. Regrettably it has been taken by many Christians to justify the 'exploitation' of nature and its resources. They have believed that humankind is free to take from the world everything that it wants without considering the long-term cost. Other religious traditions, such as Hinduism, have had much more to say about the need to respect nature than the Christian faith. It was Chief Seattle, representing the North American spiritual tradition in the mid 19th century, who said to some Americans who were trying to negotiate the sale of land from him: "Teach your children what we have taught our children, that the earth is our mother. Whatever befalls the earth befalls the children of the earth. If we spit on the ground we spit on ourselves. This we know. The earth does not belong to us; we belong to the earth… The earth is precious to God and to harm the earth is to heap contempt on the Creator."

[A] If the human race really believed that God created the world do you think it would make a difference to the way it is treated?

Talk it over

Are you more aware of human beings as the masters of nature or their weaknesses and failures?

Another way of looking

The idea of 'domination' is not, though, the last Christian word on the subject. In the opening chapters of the Bible there are two different stories of creation. In the first account everything is created before the first man and then woman are made by God. Both stand as the summit of God's creative work and it is from this that the idea of humankind dominating the earth beneath it comes. It is expressed in this way in box 1: "You made him ruler over the works of your hands, you put everything under his feet."

There is, though, another story in Genesis. In this second story man is made from the dust of the earth and placed by God in a beautiful garden. Woman is then made from a part of man's body and the two of them live together happily. Man is given the job of working in the garden and caring for it. In this way God is showing his care and concern for the whole of nature - from the greatest to the very least.

Furthermore, the responsibility of looking after the earth is passed down to all future generations. Each generation has the God-given task of being his stewards. All of the resources of the earth have been given to individuals to use for the benefit of themselves, their families and all future generations. It is a failure to appreciate this which has led to the very strong criticisms of Desmond Morris and others.

BOX 2

PSALM 24.1,2

To the Lord God belongs the earth and everything it it, the world and all its inhabitants. For it was he who founded it on the seas and planted it firm on the waters beneath.

Work to do

1 a. There are two stories of the creation of the world in the book of Genesis with rather different messages. What are the two messages?
b. When the Psalmist speaks of man being 'the master of things' what kind of mastery do you think he has in mind?

2 a. What do Christians mean when they refer to God as the 'creator' of the world?
b. What do Christians mean when they refer to God as the creator of the human race?

[B] Do you think that human beings should be 'thankful' for what the earth provides? If so, to whom?

3:13 | Damaging the World [1]

KEY QUESTION

HOW IS THE WORLD BEING DAMAGED?

By speaking of the 'environment' we are referring to the whole world in which we live and the atmosphere which surrounds it. Every part of the environment is suffering from the effects of pollution and other kinds of damage. Creating pollution is a man-made activity brought about by the way that we organise our everyday lives and conduct our business. Here are three examples of worldwide damage being caused to the environment:

Deforestation

Deforestation refers to the permanent clearing of forest, especially rainforest, areas for agriculture, settlement or other uses. Between 1985 and 1995 forest areas throughout the world were cleared at the rate of over 40 million acres a year – a clearance rate almost 100% faster than in the previous decade. Forests are now being destroyed at the rate of one million acres – an area the size of Great Britain – each week. An area the size of a football pitch is being cleared every second. This is extremely serious because:

1] Deforestation makes a considerable contribution to global warming. Carbon dioxide is the most important of the greenhouse gases which build up in the atmosphere and cause global warming [see below]. These gases trap heat warming the earth and about 20% of the carbon dioxide released on earth comes from the burning of the forests.

2] Although rainforests only cover about 6% of the earth's surface they contain 50% of all the world's species. About 5,000 species are being totally

[A] Why is deforestation a great threat to the future?

1. a. What is global warming?
   b. Why does global warming represent such a threat to the future of the human race?

2. a. What is the ozone layer?
   b. What does the ozone layer do?
   c. How is the ozone layer under threat?
   d. What will happen if we continue to damage the ozone layer?

3. a. How rapidly are the forests being destroyed?
   b. Why are the forests so important for the future of the human race?
   c. What will happen in the future if the destruction of the world's rainforests continues?

4. A 12th century mystic, Hildegarde of Bingen said: "All of creation God gives to humankind to use. If this privilege is misused, God's justice permits creation to punish humanity." Produce TWO examples from recent years which shows that pollution or destruction of the habitat causes nature 'to punish humanity'

Are you optimistic or pessimistic as you look at the future prospects of the human race. Explain your answer.

eliminated each year because of deforestation. Many of them have not even been classified or named before they are lost for ever. Many life-saving drugs are taken from plants that only grow in forest areas. The dangers to the human race in continuing down this path were spelt out in the report 'Our Common Future' [see box 2]

3] Rainforests are essential for regulating the climate and controlling flooding. In the Venezuelan mud-slides which killed thousands in 1999 deforestation was a major factor. The trees in the forest areas bound the earth together before they were uprooted and burned - with disastrous consequences.

Global warming

Our planet is surrounded by a blanket of gases which insulate it and guarantee a stable temperature in which life can survive and prosper. This blanket acts like a greenhouse around the earth but, because of pollution, the greenhouse is becoming too warm. A build-up of carbon dioxide in the atmosphere is trapping the heat radiated from the earth. During the past 100 years the overall temperature of the earth's surface has risen by almost 1%. If this trend were to continue then the ice-caps in the Antarctic and Arctic Oceans would melt and the water levels in the oceans would rise by about 1.5 metres - having catastrophic consequences for many parts of the world. Many low-lying, and inhabited, parts of the earth's surface would be inundated with water.

The Ozone Layer

Ozone in the atmosphere, formed from a small amount of oxygen, forms a layer above the earth to filter out the lethal ultraviolet rays from the sun. Over the years the use of chlorofluorocarbons [CFCs] in such appliances as refrigerator compressors and aerosols has led to the destruction of ozone molecules in the upper atmosphere'. These chlorine compounds remain active in the atmosphere for at least 100 years even though the use of most of them has now been phased out. The holes which these compounds have punched in the ozone layer will take a century or more to repair. In the meantime, people on earth are vulnerable to a whole range of health hazards from eye cataracts and skin cancer to crop damage.'

BOX 1

GRO HARLEM BRUNDTLAND, POLITICIAN

For too long we have thought of the atmosphere as a limitless good. We have been burning fuel and emitting pollutants, pressing aerosol buttons and blowing foam to our heart's content... Time has come to develop an action plan for protecting the atmosphere... Time has come to start the process of change... For too long have we neglected that we have been playing lethal games with vital life-support systems.

BOX 2

REPORT. OUR COMMON FUTURE

Species that are important to human welfare are not just wild plants or animals. Species such as earthworms, bees and termites may be far more important in terms of the role they play in a healthy and productive ecosystem. It would be grim irony indeed if just as new genetic engineering techniques begins to let us peer into life's diversity and use genes more effectively to better the human condition, we looked and found this treasure sadly depleted.

3:14 | Damaging the World [2]

The greatest threat to the environment is the way that people live. In the previous unit we looked at three problems - the greenhouse effect, the destruction of the ozone layer and deforestation - which affect people across national borders. In this unit we look at pollution on a more local level:

1] TRAFFIC In 1955 there were about 40 million cars in the world but at the beginning of the 21st century there are over 400 million - an increase of 1000% in 45 years. It is estimated that the number of cars in the UK and throughout the world will more than double between 2000 and 2025. Cars are a major source of pollution [A]. Hydrocarbons are released from petrol and sunlight acting on them produces ozone at a low level. Such ozone interferes with breathing, causing coughing and choking. Other dangerous pollutants found in petrol can cause cancer, reproductive problems and birth defects. Lead in the air can affect the learning ability of children.

2] HABITAT LOSS Since 1945 the UK has lost many of its most valuable habitats - hedgerows [150,000 miles]; wildflower meadows [95%] and ancient woodlands [50%]. Numerous species of plants and animals live in these specialised habitats - no habitats, no species.

3] WASTE The average British household disposes of a tonne of rubbish each year. Most of this rubbish is placed in landfill sites but much of the rubbish is not biodegradeable. Recycling is the only real option for the future and we will look at this in unit 3.15. Britain is now recycling about 30% of its waste paper, compared with 15% thirty years ago, but there is still a very long way to go.

4] ENERGY Everyday the sun bathes the earth with plentiful supplies of energy, without which life on earth would be impossible. Eventually, in about two billion years, the sun will die and so will life on earth. In the meantime the resources sustained by the sun - trees, plants and the animals that feed on them - will be renewable. The same is not true, though, of deposits of minerals, ores and fossil fuels, including oil, gas and coal. Such resources were laid down millions of years ago and cannot be renewed. They will eventually run out. Everyone has become increasingly aware of the dangers of relying on nuclear fuel in the future whilst the problems of disposing nuclear waste remains unsolved.

5] WATER POLLUTION For thousands of years humanity has consigned much of its waste to rivers and seas. Where settlements were small, and the amount of waste limited, little harm was done. Provided the wastes can decompose naturally and there is enough water to wash them away little long-term damage is done. But as cities have grown, and industry has increased, so the toxicity of wastes has become so much greater. Many rivers have lost the ability to clean themselves.

In recent years large quantities of pesticides and nitrates have been used on farmland in Britain to make the ground more productive - and more resistant to pests. Rain has washed these off the land into local rivers and streams. Fish have been killed in their thousands, poisoned or suffocated, and drinking water is often badly affected.

The downward path

The human race cannot continue to rush headlong down this path without suffering severe consequences. The whole of the world's fragile future life depends on maintaining a very careful

---

BOX 1

SIR JOHN LUBBOCK, 1898

The spring and the rivulet, the brook, the river and the lake, seem to give life to Nature, and were indeed regarded by our ancestors as living entities themselves. Water is beautiful in the morning mist, in the broad lake, in the glancing stream, in the river pool… beautiful in all its varied moods. The refreshing power of water upon the earth is scarcely greater than that which it exercises in the mind of man.

1 Describe THREE major causes of pollution.

2 Why is the disposal of waste such a major problem in the modern world?

3 What problems are presented by the need to provide energy supplies for the future?

4 Why are the rivers and streams of Britain, and elsewhere becoming so polluted?

5 a. Give an example of how human beings are wrecking the world.
b. What was God's purpose for human beings according to the Genesis creation story?
c. Give ONE example of how human beings are trying to save the world.

balance between the health of the earth and the needs of the human race. A large part of the answer for the future must lie in the human race adjusting its life-style so that it begins to live in harmony with nature - and not against it.

However, more than this is needed. Both governments and industry, especially multinational companies, need to change the way that they consider the earth and its resources. At the moment both are simply concerned to extract as they much as they can from what is a finite [limited] resource. Lester Brown, see box 2, points out the simple fact that this present generation is obliged to hand on to the next the world in as pure a condition as possible.

BOX 2

LESTER BROWN, AMERICAN ENVIRONMENTALIST

We have not inherited the earth from our fathers, we are borrowing it from our children.

[A] The motor-car has been described as one of the most dangerous inventions of the 20th century. Do you agree?

3:15 | Saving the Planet

KEY QUESTION

WHAT IS BEING DONE TO SAVE THE PLANET?

This planet on which 6 million people live is in a state of real crisis. The human race finds itself at a crossroads. The decisions that it makes in the next few decades about the environment will decide what kind of long-term future the planet has. Christians should be amongst those who are most concerned about the planet. Yet:

1] In its opening chapters the Bible suggests that God made the world – and then appointed man to be his steward or representative on earth. This has not prevented the human race from exploiting the earth and its resources for its own greedy ends.
2] Some of the emphases in the Bible have been deliberately exploited in the past – to the detriment of the planet's health. In particular, the idea supported by the first of the creation stories in Genesis that humanity is at the centre of the universe has led many in the past to have an inflated idea of the importance of the human race.
3] The Church has done very little over the centuries to persuade Christian worshippers to adopt a sensible life-style. Instead of encouraging a simple way of life, as was followed by Jesus, the Church has been an example of wealth and privilege. Even today it does very little to challenge the over-consumption and waste of Western

countries that is at the heart of so many of our environmental problems.

Conservation

To guarantee a long-term future for our planet conservation is essential. Whatever mistakes the human race has made in the past, and there have been many, active and drastic steps must be taken in the future. These must include:
1] The tackling of pollution. About 50% of the pollution in the atmosphere is caused by 10% of the cars on the road. Tackling this would go some way to solving the twin evils of global warming and the destruction of the ozone layer. The use of pesticides and fertilisers on the land is a crucial problem and the move towards eating more organic food is very important. We still have not found a satisfactory, and affordable, way of dealing

[A] Why do you think that people in this country do little recycling compared with other countries?

[B] A small act but do you think we could make a real difference to the planet's health if we all tried harder?

(▶) Work to do

1 The writers in extract 2 suggest that it is up to everyone, and not just governments or industry, to do something about saving the world. Do you agree with them? If so, what do you think that everyone should be doing about it?

2 a. What is recycling?
b. Why is recycling such an important part of safeguarding the planet's future?

3 Why should Christians be in the forefront of those who are fighting to save the planet?

with human sewage - most of which is dumped out at sea. Less than 10% of British beaches have come up to the highest standards of cleanliness in recent European Commission surveys.

2] An increase in recycling. Whilst 90% of all household rubbish ends up in landfill sites 7 out of every 10 household items could be recycled. Recycling paper, for instance, at home and work is something that everyone could do. For the same amount of paper produced recycling uses only 50% of the energy and a tenth of the water. It also reduces the need for intensified wood production, which harms wildlife.

3] Energy must be conserved. Both the planet, and individuals, will benefit, if steps are taken to conserve as much energy as possible. All houses should be insulated to prevent energy loss and all appliances tested for energy efficiency. Unnecessary car journeys need to be eliminated and car-sharing become a normal part of everyday life. The world needs new renewable, non-polluting sources of energy.

4] Nature should be largely left alone. Problems such as the destruction of the world's most important habitats, like rainforests, need to be tackled urgently. As these areas of rainforests are being cleared for housing and industry they are irreplaceable. On a more local level the growth of wildlife gardens and the replacement of miles of hedgerows are essential. Many wildlife species are now close to extinction because their sources of food and shelter have been taken away.

The Green Audit

Many companies are now having 'green audits' carried out to see how environmentally friendly their operations are. Amongst the issues examined in Green Audits are:

1] Whether the firm is making efficient use of the energy that it uses - where are the areas where energy is wasted? What can be done to save energy?
2] Whether the company uses many disposable products and, if so, what happens to them and how they are destroyed. Can they be re-used?
3] Whether the company has explored the possibility of using as many green products as possible and what use it makes of recycling facilities.
4] Whether the firm uses toxic products and, if so, how workers are protected from them and how they are disposed of.

BOX 1

HUGH AND MARGARET BROWN

It is easy to say that it is up to Governments and industry to put things right but, in practice, it is what we do and what we buy or reject that dictates what industry and Governments do. We are all, in some small way, responsible for what happens to the world as a whole. We can no longer ignore the fact that if each of us in our everyday life does not do something about it, we may not have a world fit to live in.

BOX 2

DAVID MCTAGGART. GREENPEACE INTERNATIONAL

Either we change now, by choice, or we change later through necessity and suffer the consequences.

3:16 | Animal Rights

Animals have been kept in captivity, and domesticated, for at least 4,000 years. Recently, however, there has been a marked change in public attitude to animals and the way that they are treated in the modern world. There are many difficult questions to ask and answer.

Treating animals today

Serious questions have been asked about the way that animals are treated today in four respects:

1] Animals in captivity. Since the mid 19th century animals have been kept in captivity [zoos] and as performers [circuses]. Due to public disquiet few circuses today use live animals. Animals are still kept in captivity in zoos but more and more the emphasis in these places is on the conservation of endangered species.

2] Animals for food. Over 150 million tonnes of meat are eaten worldwide in a year. Many people feel very unhappy about the way that animals are reared, fed and slaughtered. They become 'vegetarians' and do not eat meat of any kind. There is nothing in the Bible to suggest that eating meat is incompatible with a belief in God. Many Christians, though, are very unhappy about the way that animals are reared and so feel that they

cannot eat meat. Most people who do eat meat are beginning to ask questions about the way that the food industry treats animals. Can it be right to pen animals up and completely control their light, heat, ventilation, exercise and food intake as we do in factory farming?

3] Animals for research. Over 250 million animals a year are used in research for medical and cosmetic purposes. Much of this research is carried out without an anaesthetic being used. In this country alone 250,000 animals – including mice, rats, cats and dogs – die each year as a result of the experiments carried out on them. The supposed justification for these experiments is over-valued and much of the information could be obtained without using animals.

4] Hunting animals. People hunt and shoot animals for enjoyment. Fox-hunting and stag-hunting have been part of the English way of life for centuries.Rearing and shooting pheasants on large

[A] Find out some information about ONE organisation which works to protect some aspect of wild-life.

BOX 1

GENESIS 1.20-22

And God said, 'Let the water teem with living creatures, and let birds fly above the earth across the expanse of the sky.' So God created the great creatures of the sea and every living and moving thing with which the water teems, according to their kinds, and every winged bird according to its kind. And God saw that it was good. God blessed them and said, 'Be fruitful and increase in number and fill the water in the seas, and let the birds increase on the earth.

[B] Find out some information about the disappearance of many species of wild-life from the earth - and the danger that this presents.

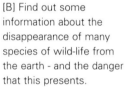

country estates is big business. Attempts to outlaw such activities have proved very controversial and at the end of the 20th century it has set many town and country people on a collision course.

From a Christian point of view

The Bible assumes that people will kill and eat animals. Amongst the many laws that God gave the Jews were those telling them how to kill and cook animals. This reflects the story of creation in the opening chapters of the Bible where we read: "And God blessed them, and God said to them, 'Be fruitful and multiply, and fill the earth and subdue it; and have dominion over the fish of the sea and over the birds of the air and over every living thing that moves upon the earth." [Genesis 1.28].

No-one has been quite sure over the centuries what the words 'subdue' and 'have dominion' were intended to mean. Later, in the creation story, human beings are described as 'stewards' of the earth and that suggests a rather different picture. A steward has delegated authority from his master to whom he is, in the end, answerable for his actions. 'Subdue' and 'dominion', however, suggest autocratic power and that is certainly how people

Talk it over

Do you think the majority of people would pay more for their food if they were sure that animals were being treated humanely?

Work to do

1 a. What is vegetarianism?
b. Why do you think that many Christians have decided to follow a vegetarian way of life?

2 a. Describe TWO ways in which the treatment of animals in the modern world causes you some/much concern.
b. Do you think that it is necessary to treat animals cruelly?
c. Is there anything in the Bible to suggest that human beings can treat animals how they wish?

3 Do you think it is worrying is people come to regard the killing of animals as a sport? Explain your answer.

have understood their power in the past. They would have done well to have remembered the prophet Isaiah who said that God is like a 'shepherd' who: "carries the lambs in his bosom and leads the ewes to water' [Isaiah 40.11.]

It is worth remembering that Jesus called himself the 'Good Shepherd' and he may well have had this passage from Isaiah in mind when he did so. It is very difficult to imagine God the Shepherd and Jesus, the Good Shepherd, approving of factory farming methods, cosmetic experiments being carried out on animals and hares and foxes being chased to a point of total exhaustion.

BOX 2

PSALM 36.6

Your righteousness is like the mighty mountains,
your justice like the great deep.
O Lord, you preserve both man and beast.
How priceless is your unfailing love!